JOYCE'S *ULYSSES*

Continuum Reader's Guides

Continuum Reader's Guides are clear, concise and accessible introductions to classic literary texts. Each book explores the themes, context, criticism and influence of key works, providing a practical introduction to close reading and guiding the reader towards a thorough understanding of the text. Ideal for undergraduate students, the guides provide an essential resource for anyone who needs to get to grips with a literary text.

Achebe's Things Fall Apart – Ode Ogede
Austen's Emma – Gregg A. Hecimovich
Bram Stoker's Dracula – William Hughes
Chaucer's The Canterbury Tales – Gail Ashton
Conrad's Heart of Darkness – Allan Simmons
Dickens's Great Expectations – Ian Brinton
Eliot's Middlemarch – Josie Billington
Fitzgerald's The Great Gatsby – Nicolas Tredell
Fowles's The French Lieutenant's Woman – William Stephenson
James's The Turn of the Screw – Leonard Orr
Salinger's The Catcher in the Rye – Sarah Graham
William Blake's Poetry – Jonathan Roberts

JOYCE'S *ULYSSES*

A READER'S GUIDE

SEAN SHEEHAN

continuum

Continuum International Publishing Group

The Tower Building	80 Maiden Lane, Suite 704
11 York Road	New York
London SE1 7NX	NY 10038

www.continuumbooks.com

British Library Cataloguing-in-Publication Data
A catalogue record for this book is available from the British Library.

ISBN: 978-1-8470-6518-6 (hardback)
            978-1-8470-6519-3 (paperback)

Library of Congress Cataloging-in-Publication Data
A catalog record for this book is available from the Library of Congress.

Typeset by Newgen Imaging Systems Pvt Ltd, Chennai, India
Printed and bound in Great Britain by MPG Books Ltd, Bodmin, Cornwall

CONTENTS

CHAPTER 1

CONTEXTS

James Joyce was born in 1882 into a middle-class Catholic Dublin family and the course of his childhood charts the family's gradual impoverishment. His father, John Stanislaus, owned property in Cork and there were servants in their Dublin home. As the final decade of the nineteenth century approached, the family moved to a new home in Bray, a suburb to the south of Dublin, and the young James was sent to the prestigious Clongowes Wood College as a boarder. Family financial problems, brought on by the father's drinking and loss of his job, soon affected James and he had to leave the school just as his family had to leave their comfortable Bray existence and move to the north side of the city. After a brief spell attending a Christian Brothers' school, John Joyce was able to get his son a free place at Belvedere College, a highly regarded Jesuit day school in Dublin, and it was here that Joyce first read Charles Lamb's *The Adventures of Ulysses*. Academically precocious, Joyce became a student at University College Dublin where he read widely and deeply and became familiar with European writers who were not on any of his reading lists. All this time his family was falling deeper into poverty. Early in 1902 he graduated with a degree in Modern Languages, a month after the death of his 14-year-old brother from typhoid fever. Joyce sang his favourite lyric, Yeats's 'Who Goes with Fergus?', at his brother's bedside.

The downfall of Charles Stewart Parnell, leader of the Irish Parliamentary Party at Westminster and champion of the Home Rule Movement, parallels the fall from prosperity for the Joyce family and provides the political landscape in which James grew up. Parnell joined forces with Gladstone's Liberal Party in return for Home Rule for Ireland. Then, at the end of the 1880s, Parnell was cited in divorce proceedings and his affair with the married Kitty O'Shea became public knowledge. The Irish Catholic Church and Gladstone denounced him, the Irish party was split and Parnell lost his position of influence. Parnell's fall was a bitter disappointment to his supporters, of whom John Joyce was one, and Irish hopes for some form of limited independence from Britain grew moribund. An age of political activism was over as the Irish Nationalist Party fragmented and a right-wing hegemony of church and state emerged to dominate Catholic Ireland. The Catholic Church in Ireland sought to contain the force of secular nationalism and was happy to collude with a British presence so long as the occupier continued to acknowledge the right of the Church to its share in the governance of the colony.

REJECTING THE IRISH REVIVAL

Political dissent shifted to a cultural front and what became known as the Irish Revival exerted a growing importance in the early decades of Joyce's life. Reconstructing the forgotten art of ballads, epics and national myths became an artistic and ideological project designed to forge a new national consciousness and members of the Anglo-Irish elite were united in their resolve to build a syncretic, intensified form of nationalist sentiment that would fuse Anglo-Irish Ireland with Irish Ireland. The Revival looked back to a mythical, pre-Christian Ireland for sources of a national identity, from athletic games to language and literature. The Irish Literary Revival, dominated by Anglo-Irish, Protestants figures, attracted Yeats, J. M. Synge, Lady Gregory, George Moore and George Russell (also known as AE). It sought to be non-sectarian but the wish to bring together the best of Anglo-Irish culture with native Gaelic forms was blind to political bloodlines. The existence of the Anglo-Irish depended on a class-based, colonial order, the result of invasion and imposition, and not everyone was unaware of this.

Joyce rejected the Irish Literary Revival and the cultural nationalism of Yeats which sought to graft an ideological layer onto forms of the Irish literary tradition buried in Gaelic myth and folklore. Colonialist stereotypes, argued revivalists, would be traduced by fresh images of Irish art intimating a collectivist spirit of community. Joyce could not identify with the kind of nationalism that the Revival espoused although he could respect its ideal of creating a literature

2

that would be Irish and modern. What he rejected was the middle-class politics of the literati and the morality of a religion that had condemned Parnell. For Joyce the Revival shared the hypocrisy of Irish Catholicism when it came to matters sexual and he distrusted the class allegiances of Anglo-Irish figures as much as he suspected their aesthetics. His model of national expression was Ibsen and in his early critical writings Joyce laments the failure of Irish writers to challenge the tradition in which they have been placed while at the same time ridiculing Anglo-Irish revivalists.

MEETING PEOPLE

Joyce had registered to study medicine in Dublin after graduating but he left Ireland in late 1902 for Paris where the Faculté de Médecine offered him a place. He returned sooner than expected when his mother became seriously ill in April 1903. The telegram that arrived from his father read: 'Nother [sic] dying, come home father.' She died in August, after pleading unsuccessfully with her eldest son to return to Catholicism, and Joyce was still in Ireland the following year when, on 16 June 1904, he first walked out with Nora Barnacle, a young woman he had met on Nassau Street in Dublin. She was 20, came from Galway in the west of Ireland and was feisty enough to have left home after her uncle beat her for consorting with a young Protestant man. Uneducated, having left school at the age of 12, she found employment in a Dublin hotel as a chambermaid. She won the heart of the would-be writer who wrote to her of his profound dissatisfaction with Ireland – 'There is no life here – no naturalness or honesty. People live together in the same houses all their lives and at the end they are as far apart as ever'[1] and in October 1904 they left for the continent where Joyce had got a job teaching English. Emigration was nothing new for the Irish: saints and scholars had been travers-ing Europe since the end of the Roman Empire, joined by political exiles from the sixteenth century onwards, and Joyce saw himself as part of an honourable tradition. A number of militant nationalists, the Fenians, had fled to Paris over the years, including a Joseph Casey whom the young Joyce met there through his father's connections. Named Egan in chapter three of *Ulysses* – the fictional Stephen Dedalus has spent time with him – Casey is remembered with affection (see page 32). Someone else whom Joyce remembered, though not with affection, was Oliver St John Gogarty, a wealthy and well-connected medical student at Trinity College. Joyce had met Gogarty during the period in Dublin after his mother's death and, for a brief time, they shared accommodation in a disused defensive tower built by the military to the south of Dublin's city centre. In *Ulysses* Gogarty becomes Mulligan and the tower serves as the location for most of the novel's first chapter.

There was an incident that occurred shortly after Joyce first met Nora that would later make a vital contribution to the inspiration for *Ulysses*. Joyce got seriously drunk one night and angered a young man by making advances towards his girlfriend. Joyce was beaten up and left on the street and it seems likely that it was on this occasion that he was helped by a stranger, an apparently Jewish Dubliner with an unfaithful wife, and taken home. The stranger, whose name was Hunter, would become the fictional Leopold Bloom and in *Ulysses* he would help Stephen Dedalus and bring him back to his home after he was punched to the ground by a British soldier.

TRIESTE AND ZURICH

Joyce and Nora, after a brief spell in Pola and later in Rome, settled down to life in Trieste. A child, named Giorgio after Joyce's dead brother George, was born in 1905 and a daughter, Lucia, the following year. Multicultural Trieste, an outpost of the Austrian–Hungarian empire, boasted diverse languages and, like Dublin, bristled with colonial dissatisfaction. Joyce enjoyed the city's lively cosmopolitanism, mixing with its Jewish and socialist communities and embracing new forms of art such as the cinema. In 1909 he persuaded some businesspeople to invest in cinemas in Ireland but the project failed even though Joyce had returned to Dublin and established the first one in the Irish capitol. From the articles he wrote for a Trieste nationalist newspaper and from lectures he gave at the local university, it is clear that Joyce was giving thought to the political and cultural issues facing Irish people. The country's colonial status was a given, it was futile to rail against its injustice because this was in the nature of empire, wrote Joyce, and an independence of mind was necessary to defeat the forces of reaction, which included the Catholic church as much as the British political order. He welcomed the emergence of Sinn Féin as a new force in Irish nationalism.

Joyce remembered his mother and he had written to Nora in 1904: 'When I looked on the face as she lay in her coffin – a face grey and wasted with cancer – I understood that I was looking on the face of a victim and I cursed the system which had made her a victim.'[2] It was in 1904 that Joyce began a set of short stories that became *Dubliners* and a sense of victimhood characterizes their mood, sharpened by an acute sense of how colonialism has sapped the moral fibre of a people. This was brought home when the Dublin publisher who agreed to bring the stories out began to have qualms, asking for changes lest he be prosecuted (words like 'bloody' worried him), and it was 1914 before the book was published. The author was dismayed and when the poet Ezra Pound expressed interest in his writing Joyce sent him the first chapter of *A Portrait of the Artist as a Young Man*, a novel he had started in 1907 and which emerged from an earlier autobiographical work called *Stephen Hero*.

A new chapter in Joyce's life began with the outbreak of World War I and hostilities between Italy and Austria. His brother Stanislaus, who had moved to Trieste, was interned in 1915 – Britain was also at war with Italy – and it seemed wise to decamp. They settled in Zurich, from where Joyce heard news of the Easter Rising when an armed band of nationalists and socialists took over key buildings in the Irish capital and from outside the General Post Office declared Ireland to be an independent Republic. The mass executions that followed the suppression of the revolt would in time help ignite a more sustained rejection of British rule. By this year, 1916, Joyce had written the first chapter of *Ulysses* and although the novel would be finished back in Trieste and then Paris, the bulk of the novel took shape in neutral Zurich, a city where Lenin was also seeking refuge from the war. *Ulysses* is set in 1904 but was written in 1914–21, years when Dublin was the centre of anti-colonial resistance to British rule. Joyce heard of the 1916 shelling of the city centre by British troops at the very time he was writing about the same streets, giving a twist to his much-quoted remark that if Dublin was destroyed it could be rebuilt using *Ulysses* as a guide. Armed resistance to British rule resurfaced in 1919 and two years later, following a truce and peace talks, a treaty was signed that gave Ireland (but not six counties in Ulster) a degree of independence but not the status of a republic. This led to an Irish civil war between pro- and anti-Treaty parties.

The years of writing *Ulysses*, involving twenty different addresses over three countries, were incredibly unsettled ones for the Joyce family. Joyce was making new friends, like Frank Budgen in Zurich, and enjoying late nights in the bars but all the time he was intently focused on the writing of his novel. He wrote letters to his aunt Josephine in Dublin, a sister of his mother, asking for data and details needed for his novel. He wanted to know, for the chapter where Bloom, the novel's central character, brings the young Stephen Dedalus back to his home only to find he has no front door key, whether an average person could climb over the area railings of 7 Eccles Street (17.84–9). Joyce craved the ephemeral as well as the empirical, asking his aunt for Dublin gossip and copies of local newspapers.

Ireland provided Joyce with everything he needed for his novel, including the existence of a small Jewish community in Dublin which gave him the basis for the partly alienated identity of his fictional hero as an Irish Jew. The otherness of Leopold Bloom, the central character in *Ulysses*, is represented by his Jewishness and it has a historical root in the anti-semitic pogrom that broke out in Limerick in 1904. Jewish immigrants had first arrived in Ireland in the 1880s, fleeing persecution in Russia, and they encountered anti-semitism as well as a contrary tradition that identified the Irish and Jews as fellow-victims of oppression and diaspora. The division in attitude became apparent in the Irish nationalist movement, with some figures attacking Jews for all their stereotyped faults and others identifying with them and their history.

It was in Trieste that Joyce first got to know Jews personally and here too he deepened his awareness of nineteenth-century anti-semitic discourses and its process of stereotyping Jews. This awareness reveals itself constantly in the novel, not just through the anti-semitic remarks of Haines and Mr Deasy in the first two chapters but by the day's constant reminders for Bloom that he is perceived by others as a 'Jew'. He is Irish but also, through Hungarian extraction on his father's side, Jewish – a pluralist assimilation that enables him to enjoy pork kidney for breakfast – though his father converted to Protestantism and adopted the name Bloom instead of the Hungarian Virag. Bloom does not forget his Jewish heritage. He keeps his father's *Haggadah*, a religious text fulfilling a Jew's scriptural obligation to tell of Jewish liberation from slavery in Egypt, and the suicide note that his father addressed to him. Throughout the day, Bloom is reminded of his father's plight as an immigrant Jew in Ireland. He endures in silence, anti-semitic remarks by the fellow Dubliners whose company he shares in a carriage journey for the

funeral of a mutual acquaintance but later in the day publicly declares
and defends his Jewishness in a pub. Allusions to Jewishness permeate his fantasies in the 'Circe' chapter, indicative of his deep-rooted
anxiety on the subject, and it is pertinent to note how Joyce wanted
to emphasize this by adding, at a late stage to the page proofs, how in
the apparition of Bloom's dead young son, Rudy, the child is seen
reading from right to left before he kisses the page of the book he
is reading. In the 'Eumaeus' chapter, towards the end of the novel,
Bloom asserts his agnosticism and tells Stephen he is not a Jew, which
is true in the sense that he does not subscribe to the beliefs or practices of any religion, while also expressing his sense of the injustices
inflicted on Jews through history. Tellingly, in the penultimate chapter of *Ulysses* Bloom embraces his Jewishness in a movement of
conciliation that mirrors his acceptance of the infidelity committed
that day by his wife Molly.

There is another parallel at work in the novel, between Bloom's
troubled ethnicity and Stephen's engagement with Irish Catholicism,
that sees both Bloom and Stephen struggling with the task of estab-
lishing an identity within a cultural tradition from which they feel
alienated. They are both outsiders: in the 'Nausicaa' chapter Bloom
recalls how Molly chose him because 'you were so foreign from the
others' (13.1210) and the young woman who observes him on the
beach in that chapter registers him as 'that foreign gentleman'
(13.1302). In the first chapter, Stephen Dedalus declares that he is the
servant of two masters, the Vatican and the British state (1.638), and
in a later chapter he points to his head as the place where he must
'kill the priest and the king' (15.4437). The otherness of Bloom as an
Irish Jew and of Stephen as an iconoclast who rejects British imperial
rule and Catholicism blend in pointing towards an aspect of Joyce
that distinguishes him from many of his fellow modernists. Pound,
Yeats and Eliot shared disturbingly right-wing views but Joyce, who
was drawn to libertarian socialism as a young man, is a left-wing
maverick by comparison and Bloom's Jewishness has as much a
political as an aesthetic presence in *Ulysses*.

LIFE AFTER *ULYSSES*

Joyce's own alienation from Ireland ensured that he and his family
returned to Trieste after the end of World War I and when it became

clear that the city had lost its appeal for them, they planned to settle in London. As it happened, Paris detained them en route and the city became their home for the next 20 years. During these years Joyce's financial affairs were placed on a better footing than ever before, mainly due to the assistance of Harriet Shaw Weaver, a wealthy Englishwoman with an interest in avant-garde literature. Weaver had brought out *A Portrait* in 1917 and as editor of *The Egoist* magazine was publishing episodes of *Ulysses*. Another woman, Sylvia Beach, who owned a Paris bookshop and who met Joyce there, also became an important person in his life and she became the first publisher of *Ulysses*.

It was in Paris that Joyce became a famous literary figure, thanks in no small part to the influence of Pound, and received visitors like T. S. Eliot. By 1921 *Ulysses* was in theory ready for printing but Joyce worked furiously on the page proofs and the book grew in size by a third before it was published in 1922.

Nora Joyce wanted to revisit Ireland and she travelled back to Galway in 1922 with her children, in the throes of a civil war which came dangerously close when the train she was travelling on back to Dublin came under fire from anti-Treaty forces; Joyce was terrified for their safety. Even when the civil war was over, Joyce had no inclination to return to an Ireland that had settled into becoming a Church-dominated and conservative country. His interest in the country and its people remained a constant, though, as throughout his life and in Paris he loved receiving visitors from Ireland who could bring him news.

Joyce's sense of alienation from Ireland, inseparable from his love of the place, did not change with the country's coming of independence in the years after the civil war. The anti-Treaty party adopted parliamentary tactics and won electoral power in 1932 and in that year Yeats and G. B. Shaw proposed an Academy of Irish Letters. Joyce politely but firmly rejected an invitation to join, remaining hostile to Anglo-Irish cultural politics. Joyce died in Zurich in 1941. When it was suggested to his wife that a priest conduct a religious funeral Nora refused, saying in effect that she could not betray her husband by agreeing to such a thing. The feeling of hostility between Joyce and Catholic Ireland was mutual, with the Irish government declining to send a representative to his funeral (although the country had two diplomats in Switzerland) and De Valera, the Irish prime minister at the time, only wanted to know if Joyce had died a Catholic. It was left to a British minister to deliver an address at the cemetery: 'Of all the injustices Britain has heaped upon Ireland', he said, 'Ireland will continue to enjoy the lasting revenge of producing masterpieces of English literature.'[3]

CHAPTER 2

LANGUAGE, STYLE AND FORM

Despite the novel's length, some 260,000 words, the plot of *Ulysses* is not difficult to summarize. It is based on one day in Dublin, Thursday 16 June 1904, and follows two main characters, middle-aged Leopold Bloom and young Stephen Dedalus, as they make their way around Dublin from 8 a.m. until 2 a.m. Their paths cross more than once but it is only at night, as a result of the older man helping young Stephen after his drunken altercation with a British soldier, that they finally talk to one another. Bloom takes him home and makes cocoa for them while his wife, Molly, lies upstairs in bed. Stephen then leaves and Bloom joins his wife in bed. Despite the simple plotline, difficulties arise for most readers who start reading *Ulysses* without some assistance from the kind of commentary offered in the next chapter and the novice may find some comfort in knowing that Virginia Woolf resorted to noting down some very ordinary facts to help steer her way through the text – 'Stephen Dedalus – the son of Mr Dedalus/Mulligan is his friend' – and she wondered, incorrectly, if Bloom was a newspaper editor.[1] In a later age, Bob Dylan also experienced difficulty making sense of the book when he was given a first-edition copy: 'I couldn't make hide nor hair of it.'[2] The total lack of quotation marks presents an initial problem – Joyce had no time for what he called 'perverted commas'[3] – but is readily overcome once it is realised that Joyce uses the 2-em dash (——) instead.

GENETIC CONCERNS

The challenge of reading *Ulysses* is bound up with the way it was written and its genetic history as a text. Joyce first conceived the idea for a *Dubliners* story to be called 'Ulysses' in 1906, based on an incident that had occurred two years earlier when a Dublin Jew had helped the young James Joyce by taking him home to rest and recover after a drunken night out that had ended in violence (see page 4). The short story never got off the ground but the idea for a story developed and by 1914 Joyce was ready to start writing a novel, one that was conceived at the time as more of a sequel to *A Portrait of the Artist as a Young Man* than a modern treatment of Homer's *Odyssey*. Joyce worked on his novel for a number of years, from late 1914 until October 1921, and as it evolved he returned to his text, revising and supplementing it with new material – a process that continued even after episodes of the book had been serialized – but it remains the case that there is a noticeable difference between the writing of the early and late chapters. A conventional third-person narrative using realistic dialogue and interior monologue characterizes the early chapters but by the time of the 'Cyclops' episode, chapter twelve, it plays second fiddle to radical developments – distortions might be more accurate – in the narrative form. Between chapters six and twelve one can broadly say that in terms of language and form elements of what is to come share textual space with what has gone before.

In the first six chapters, as Stephen and Bloom go about reflecting on their experiences and interpreting the external world they seem to be each in possession of a stable core of selfhood but as the writing of *Ulysses* continues there is less concern with the psychological development of the characters and the style of the these early chapters is not maintained. The change is gradual, though, because even in the early chapters it is not difficult to find Joyce working with language in new ways. In the book's second episode, 'Proteus', Stephen recalls his dream of the night before, featuring Haroun al Raschid, a caliph of Baghdad, holding a melon against his face: 'I am almosting it. That man led me, spoke '(366–7). Joyce's friend, Frank Budgen, expressed surprise at the grammatical transgression of 'almosting' but was assured: '"Yes," said Joyce. "That's all in the Protean character of the thing. Everything changes: land, water, dog, time of day. Parts of speech change, too. Adverb becomes verb."'[4] It is as if Joyce wants the language of an episode to be shaped by its subject matter, its linguistic orbit to be curved by the gravitational force of the episode's concerns. Something similar happens with the floral language and the tea motif in a passage from chapter five (see pages 37–8) the 'Lotus Eaters' episode.

A clear difference that does emerge from chapter six onwards is the increasing hypostatization of Dublin, with the city itself becoming an integral part of what the book is about. The narrative voice also shows signs of development after chapter six, becoming less objective, more ironic and playful. In chapter eight, 'Lestrygonians', for example, Bloom is hungry and preoccupied with food and this accounts for observations of his like that of a possible relationship between diet and the writing of poetry (8.543–7). The references to food, though, are so multiple and varied as to go beyond the bounds of psychological verisimilitude. When he spots John Howard Parnell on the street, looking uncannily like his dead brother Charles Parnell, his mournful demeanour prompts the thought: 'Eaten a bad egg. Poached eyes on ghost' (8.508). Is Bloom as witty as this or does the conceit emanate from a mischievous narrator who has somehow infiltrated Bloom's consciousness? At the start of the following chapter, set in the National Library, the footsteps of the librarian are described: 'He came a step a sinkapace forward on neatsleather creaking and a step backward a sinkapace on the solemn floor' (9.5–6). There are allusions to *Twelfth Night* (I.iii.136–9) and *Julius Caesar* (I.i.26–9), very apposite given the importance of Shakespeare in this chapter, and the librarian's mincing footwork reflects his tendency to fatuousness just as the library floor is seen to imbue itself with the quality of his gravely elegant utterance. A tone of derision is just below the surface and the cleverness of the description far exceeds the requirements for an impartial narrator.

It is not possible to point to one chapter and definitely assert that an abrupt change in the form of the novel has occurred. For some readers chapter ten, 'Wandering Rocks' marks the change, made up as it is of a series of short scenes linked by various interpolations and the street geography of Dublin, and the fact that Bloom and Stephen have no privileged role in what occurs. The fugue-like beginning to the next episode, 'Sirens', announces another radical departure from the traditional form of the novel but it could be argued that the sub-headings back in 'Aeolus' constitute a similar assault on the conventions of classic realist fiction. Despite the fact that something new is happening with language in 'Sirens' the chapter also has plenty of naturalistic dialogue and Bloom's interior monologue as he sits in the Ormond Bar is central to what is happening. This, after all, is the hour of the day when his wife will commit adultery and Bloom is all too aware of this fact.

TEXTUAL DISCOMFORTS

Even though there is a recognizable narrative voice in chapter twelve, 'Cyclops', that of a Dublin bar-fly with the appropriate argot, the reader's attention is arrestingly drawn to the episode's parodies, generated by chance remarks, that intrude into the text. Various discourses are the subject matter of the parodies – newspaper-style reports, baby talk, children's books, the language of epics and the Bible – and they expand alarmingly to become discomforting if comical obstacles to any normative reading of fiction. In the penultimate chapter, 'Ithaca' the style is defined by an unemotional encyclopaedism that stretches to breaking point conventional notions of realism and character. Bloom prepares to make a hot drink for Stephen and himself and a question is posed: 'What in water did Bloom, waterlover, drawer of water, watercarrier, returning to the range admire?' (17.183–4). Rather than quote the answer it is shorter to give one critic's paraphrase:

> [an] answer of 450 words, praising water for its universality, democratic equality, vastness, profundity, restlessness; the independence of its units; its variability, quiescence, turgidity, substance, sterility; its climatic and social significance, preponderance, capacity to dissolve and hold in solution; its erosion, weight, volume and density: its imperturbability, gradation of its colours, ramifications, violence, circumterrestrial curve, secrecy, latent humidity; the simplicity of its composition; its healing virtues, buoyancy, and penetrativeness; 'its infallibility as paradigm and paragon'; its metamorphoses, strength, variety of forms, solidity, docility, utility, potentiality, submarine fauna and fauna, ubiquity and 'the noxiousness of its effluvia' in marshes and stagnant pools.[5]

What becomes increasingly clear as *Ulysses* progresses is the palpable intention to draw attention to the novel's own material status as writing and to shift the reader's perspective away from a traditional concern with narrative and character development. There is a flaunting of different styles of writing that works to subvert the conventional role of the reader; initially drawn into the minds of the characters of Stephen and Bloom by the stream of consciousness technique, the reader is led by displays of stylistic bravado into a linguistic playground where one game seems to follow another. The verbal frolics that undermine notions of intersubjectivity first become obtrusive in the seventh chapter and continue apace. The final result can be heard in *Ulysses* in the roars and ripples of laughter that mock and subvert much of what passed for creditable cultural forms, in the astonishing historical exactitude and topographical verisimilitude of the book and in a hero, Leopold Bloom who is an advertising canvasser in Dublin with a Jewish father. Bloom walks out of his house on the day that Joyce first walked out with Nora Barnacle, but romantic sensibilities are dented by this also being the day on which Molly Bloom will commit adultery. Bloom has to grapple with this treachery just as, in the first three chapters, Stephen has to contend with the treacheries of history, a nightmare from which he is trying to awake.

The source of the novel's 'difficulty' is Joyce's concern with the materiality of language. The book becomes a self-reflexive, carnivesque work combining a heteroglossic style with innovative narrative strategies and stylistic aberrations. Like the Norman Foster bank in Hong Kong and its architectural ilk – with the building's style seen in its exoskeleton and the absence of any internal supporting structure – Joyce turns language inside out and exposes how it is held up. The orchestration of stylistic exercises within the text becomes inseparable from a growing self-delight at the results of holding language in front of fun-house mirrors; and the effect of reading parts of some of the later chapters is to suggest an author quirkiness that undermines the normative standards of novel reading. The effect of intertextuality in *Ulysses*, the intentional presence or echo of other texts within it, tends to have a similar effect. The normal referencing of words to things is destabilized by citing other words, other verbal references, not in order to defer to an authority but to open up new possibilities for articulation. Any established, hierarchical boundary between language and the world dissolves into an intertextual, porous landscape peopled by references, quotations, echoes, parallels and other contagious linkages. The use of Homer's *Odyssey* is the supreme example of intertextuality in Joyce.

Beckett, writing of Joyce in 1929, draws a distinction between conventional narrative structures and the foregrounding of form that characterizes *Ulysses*:

You [the reader] are not satisfied unless form is so strictly divorced from content that you can comprehend the one almost without bothering to read the other. This rapid skimming and absorption of the scant cream of sense is made possible by what I may call a continuous process of copious intellectual salivation.[6]

Joyce expressed a similar understanding when he wrote to Harriet Weaver in 1919:

I understand that you may begin to regard the various styles of the episodes with dismay and prefer the initial style much as the wanderer did who longed for the rock of Ithaca. But in the compass of one day to compress all these wanderings and clothe them in the form of this day is for me possible only by such variation which, I beg you to believe, is not capricious.[7]

SCHEMAS AND SCAFFOLDING

Joyce knew he was producing a new kind of literature and that readers and critics would need some assistance in appreciating his achievement. He produced two, broadly similar schemas for *Ulysses*, the first of which was sent to Carlo Linati in 1920 and has come to be known by his surname. Valery Larbaud borrowed it the following year and with the help of Sylvia Beach it was circulated during the 1920s. Stuart Gilbert published a slightly different version in *James Joyce's "Ulysses"* in 1930. The Linati scheme appears as an appendix in Richard Ellmann's *Ulysses on the Liffey* (1972) and the second one, known as the Gilbert scheme, can be found in the introduction to the Penguin edition of *Ulysses*. The schemas show how the relationship between the novel and Homer's *Odyssey* work at different levels. Structurally, there are three parts to the novel (a tripartite division first mentioned by Joyce in relation to his novel in 1920): the first three chapters, known as the Telemachia (from the traditional term for the first of three divisions in the *Odyssey*), can be seen, like the early episodes in Homer, as the search of a young man for his father; chapters four through fifteen, the middle section of the novel, parallel the wanderings and adventures of Homer's Odysseus as Bloom busily makes his way around Dublin; the final three chapters, known as the Nostos (from the Greek for homecoming), evoke Odysseus's return home to Ithaca, his meeting with his son Telemachus and wife Penelope and his slaying of the suitors.

In the letter to his American attorney in which Joyce first mentioned the tripartite division of his novel,[8] he also included chapter titles taken from episodes of the *Odyssey*. These titles were dropped by Joyce just before the printing of the novel, although they are the basis of the Linati and Gilbert schemas. Ulysses, the Roman name for Odysseus, was kept as the novel's title although this choice may only reflect the fact that this was a common name for the Greek hero at the time Joyce was writing. The schemas, between them, allocate scenes to episodes ('The Tavern' for 'Cyclops', 'The Brothel' for 'Circe' and so on), a time of the day, an organ, an art, colour, symbol and technique. Much has been made of these correspondences by some readers and the idea of a complex plan underlying the multifaceted material has encouraged an army of critics to engineer their own scaffolding for the text (see Chapter 4).

Joyce told his friend Frank Budgen in Zurich that

> my book is the epic of the human body . . . . In my book the body lives in and moves through space and is the home of a full human personality. The words I write are adapted to express first one of its functions then another.[9]

When Budgen questioned this by wondering how it allowed for the interiority of the characters Joyce replied, 'If they had no body they would have no mind. It's all one.'[10] Some such holistic notion is useful for the reader coming to *Ulysses* with the knowledge that a mountain of critical books have been written about how best to interpret Joyce's novel. The schemas and the scaffolding erected by critics are perhaps best treated in the manner Wittgenstein advised for his own propositions: 'anyone who understands me eventually recognises them as nonsensical, when he has used them – as steps – to climb up beyond them. (He must, so to speak, throw away the ladder after he has climbed up it.)'[11]

STYLISH REVENGE

The Homeric correspondences and other patterns that may be discerned in the book only go so far: 'it is my revolt against the English conventions, literary and otherwise, that is the main source of my talent. I don't write in English.'[12] Joyce defines himself in the negative. As an artist and intellectual writing in a period of a developing English cultural nationalism, in which the country's literary tradition was central, Joyce takes up an opposing, revengeful position. In the first three chapters this dissent is associated with Stephen Dedalus and his sullen distrust of those around him but there is a limit to how far Joyce can go with him in this direction. Stephen feels trapped, surrounded by usurpers, and he struggles in darkness for some way out of his situation. At the level of character, with Leopold Bloom coming on the scene in chapter four, a fresh prospect of resistance appears; he is Irish but also Jewish, resistant to the bigotry that has so informed the history of colonial Ireland as to become part of the nationalist consciousness among those who espouse the purity of the Gael. Bloom is part of a Dublin civic community and a supporter of Parnell but as an outsider he can also look askance at his community and much of the humour of *Ulysses* derives from Bloom's take on his fellow citizens and their lifestyle. Bloom is an outsider because he is treated as primarily a Jew by nearly all of his fellow Dubliners, even though he is uncircumcised. What helps make him intrinsically different is his secularism and his socialism: 'Free money, free rent, free love and a free lay church in a free lay state' (15.1693).

Joyce had to go deeper in his cultural war against Britain and in ways that one of his novel's characters, however critical and outré his perspective, could not achieve. It was on the field of language itself that battle would take place and so, around and through the presence of Bloom, Joyce weaves a variety of styles of English. This process becomes increasingly clear in the later chapters of the book as Joyce unpicks various English discourses that, as ways of defining what is speakable, were becoming a part of colonial Ireland through the education system, the print media and popular culture. He takes a particular discourse and overwrites it, as a palimpsest and in its own style, in such a way as to reveal the form and render it powerless. So, for example, 'Nausicaa' is adulterated with the language of women's magazines and popular newspapers, 'Circe' materializes the colonized unconscious while 'Ithaca' dematerializes the language of British empirical science. At one stage in the debate in the National Library in chapter nine, where Anglo-Irish bardolatry is under scrutiny, Stephen laughs 'to free his mind from his mind's bondage' (9.1016) and the whole of *Ulysses* can be read as one long and contented laugh at having mastered forms of English. 'I'd like a language which is above all languages . . . I cannot express myself in English without enclosing myself in a tradition.'[13] There is no tradition for the last chapter, 'Penelope', suitably devoted to an authentic female voice, a discourse that up to then had been necessarily relegated by the hierarchical order, one capable of questioning masculinity and going beyond petty nationalisms to assert a healthy outlook on life unstained by either British or Catholic mores.

The 'Oxen of the Sun' chapter parodies anthologized forms of English prose but the term parody by itself is inadequate even though its implication of some order of fidelity to that which is being mimicked, a recognition of paternity, is relevant to what Joyce is doing. What is also happening is a sabotaging of authority, a desire to transgress in order to remove the anxiety of being positioned within the tradition of English literature, of Englishness. Joyce is writing in English and this complicity is recognized but so too is the freedom to violate it through an act of unveiling – through a comedy of styles.

The eclectic styles of *Ulysses* are wide-ranging enough to also contain and encompass the classical achievement of Homer; part of Joyce's 'epic' intention being to enclose Homerism just as it encloses so many other styles and discourses. This way of relating Homer to *Ulysses*, viewing the latter as a kind of transmitter on many varied frequencies, including a Homeric one, is closely paralleled by the way Homer himself was viewed by the eighteenth-century Italian thinker Giambattista Vico (1668–1744). The relationship between Vico and Joyce is usually invoked in reference to *Finnegans Wake* but, according to Ellmann, Joyce's reading of this philosopher was already established in 1913–14, the time when he was ready to begin *Ulysses*.[14]

According to Vico, Homer is not a unique author but a kind of poetical 'character' who unites and articulates the cultural repertoire of his society, including the linguistic level: 'The Greek cities vied for the honour of claiming Homer as their own because in his epics they found words, phrases, and dialectical forms which belonged to their own vernaculars.'[15] It is this ability to expropriate discourses that allows Joyce to encompass Homer as one among many of his stylistic ingredients. It has also been clearly shown how the idea of striving to emulate Homer, of aspiring to the Homeric ideal, was a Victorian cliché.[16] A line of Andrew Lang's poem became famous – 'The surge and thunder of the Odyssey' – and it serves as a summary of what the Victorians admired in Homer: a wild beauty, something immense and infinite, energetic yet grand; virile heroes that are magical and thoroughly un-Victorian. Joyce, 19 years old when Queen Victoria died, grew up learning to loathe and reject much of what passed for this kind of Establishment culture. Far from turning to Homer in the way that T. S. Eliot suggested (see pages 85–7), it is more likely that he sought to undermine and topple just such a figure of High Culture. This is not to deny the importance of Homer's epic as a central structural support for the narrative in *Ulysses* but it does undermine the significance that T. S. Eliot attached to it.

For a long time Joyce was read as a stylist in a purist, apolitical sense and in terms of ideological force this was a sanitized Joyce elevated to a prime seat in High Modernism. The de-canonizing of this Joyce began in the 1980s (see page 95) when the idea began to dawn that, far from aligning himself with the English literary tradition and seeking to place his avant-gardism within it, Joyce wrote from the realization that he was dispossessed of such a tradition and by remaining outside it, undermining the discursive grammars of a dominant culture, its power and influence would be weakened.

ENJOYING *ULYSSES*

It is Joyce's stylistic iconoclasm, his adventures with language, his humour and the myriad ways in which *Ulysses* engages with and enlaces Irish culture and history that provide the sustaining interest in reading and re-reading the novel. The different ways of studying *Ulysses*, like the different styles and discursive formations within it, are sometimes antinomic, coming into existence as the result of attitudinal shifts in perspective. The book's protean nature ensures there is no 'true' reading waiting to be discovered but this does not mean that something truthful cannot be inscribed: the fact is that 7 Eccles Street was empty in 1904 (Joyce chose the address for that reason) and this gives some 'truth' to the fiction of having Leopold and Molly Bloom live there. It could have been like this: hence the letter to his aunt Josephine, referred to earlier, asking

> is it possible for an ordinary person to climb over the railings of no 7 Eccles Street, either from the path or the steps, lower himself down from the lowest part of the railings till his feet are within two feet or three of the ground and drop unhurt?[17]

Joyce is well known for the recherché quality of many of his references but empiricism of this kind could hardly – the pun is unavoidable – be more down-to-earth.

While notions of realism, plot and character risk seeming like flotsam washed up by the high tide of fashionable theory and left to dry on the beaches of academia, it is worth remembering that in *Ulysses* Joyce never abandoned realism, his storyline or his characters. Even in a chapter like 'Ithaca', where a certain style of writing seems more important than events in a narrative, the poignancy and loneliness of Bloom and Stephen touches the reader just as deeply, if not more so, than some of the early chapters written in 'the initial style'.

> In fact everything that Joyce does to re-realize Bloom – mythologizing him as Odysseus, Elijah, and the ghost in Hamlet, breaking up and reassembling the letters of his name, and finally abandoning his stream of consciousness, with its staccato rhythm and fireworks of wit, for the gradgrinding pedantry of 'Ithaca' – all this verbal sabotage only makes the hero more real and more loveable.[18]

Often it is best to step back from the theory and enjoy the way Joyce writes. Examples are plentiful, like the description of Mulligan on the street – 'Primrosevested he greeted gaily with his doffed Panama as with a bauble' (9.489–90) – where the character is seen playing, as with a toy, with the superficial image of his self, confirming the suspicion first aired in 'Telemachus' that, as someone lacking an ethical centre, he will instinctively fulfil the role that an occasion and his ego demands. Sometimes there is a lyrical beauty to the language that speaks for itself, like the description of the night sky in 'Ithaca': 'The heaventree of stars hung with humid nightblue fruit' (17.1039). Joyce's humour is a constant and is often to be appreciated for its own sake, without feeling the need to justify or explain it. Thus, the description of a can of sardines in the style of Mandeville (14.149–54) or the gleeful intertextuality of Bloom quoting *Hamlet* – 'For this relief much thanks' (13.939–40) – after masturbating in 'Nausicaa'. In 'Eumaeus', as Stephen and Bloom pass close to Rourke's bakery on their way towards the cabman's shelter, the reader is told how Stephen is thinking of Ibsen while Bloom smells bread: 'Bread, the staff of life, earn your bread, O tell me where is fancy bread, at Rourke's the baker's it is said.' (16.58–9) There is an echo of a song from *The Merchant of Venice* ('Tell me where is fancy bred, / Or in the heart or in the head?') but the temptation that needs resisting is to see in this some subtle comment on the differences between Stephen and Bloom. Yes, their imaginations are seen to be responding in very different ways to the same phenomena but it may be that the Shakespeare allusion is there for the making and Joyce could not help but put it in. Just as, probably, he could not resist having Bloom, listening to the fine voice of Simon Dedalus singing in the bar, think how 'tenors get women by the score' (11.686). The pun may not consciously be in Bloom's mind but Joyce would have relished it in the same spirit as he enjoyed finding a use for vernacular expressions like 'agonising Christ, wouldn't it give you a heartburn on your arse?' (7.241) or 'I was blue mouldy for the want of that pint. Declare to God I could hear it hit the pit of my stomach with a click' (12.242–3). 'The pity is', said Joyce, 'the public will demand and find a moral in my book, or worse they may take it in some serious way, and on the honour of a gentleman, there is not one single serious line in it.'[19] This is not as flippant as it may seem but rather a way of stating his determined opposition to the presumptions of any cultural establishment that would circumscribe his writing:

> In writing one must create an endlessly changing surface, dictated by the mood and current impulse in contrast to the fixed mood of the classical style . . . . The important thing is not what we write, but how we write, and in my opinion the modern writer must be an adventurer above all, willing to take every risk, and be prepared to founder in his effort if need be. In other words we must write dangerously.[20]

Ulysses has been written about, dissected and analysed so often and from so many theoretical perspectives that the reader, although coming to the novel for the first time, may have to bear the burden of some of this literary baggage. One way to lighten the load is to bear in mind Joyce's warning about taking it too seriously and to recall the way he saw himself as a writer, adventurously journeying like Odysseus into uncharted waters and taking the risks this entailed. He needed to write 'dangerously' because the times demanded a break with the past; the reward, as the novelist Ali Smith realises, is the thrill that comes in its wake:

> I was ecstatic with *Ulysses*'s play and peripatetics, its mischievousness, its bravado, its everyday greatness and great everydayness,

and its positivity, its enormous yes. It seemed to me the obvious proof that the modernist period, which at the time critics were determined to see as a period of lack and loss and dislocation and ghosts and eliotic fragmentation and despair, was at least equally a time of great and sheer energy and life and florescence – bloom even – in literary form.[21]

CHAPTER 3

READING *ULYSSES*

TELEMACHUS

Time

8 a.m.

Place

Martello tower (a circular masonry fort) on the coast at Sandycove, a few miles south of Dublin.

Plot

Buck Mulligan, a medical student, Stephen Dedalus, the aspiring artist of Joyce's *A Portrait of the Artist as a Young Man*, and Haines, a nondescript Englishman from Oxford, are preparing for the day. After breakfast and the arrival of a woman delivering milk, the three of them visit a local swimming spot before a disgruntled Stephen leaves for the school where he works.

Discussion

The first paragraph of *Ulysses* has an inviting clarity, a beguiling matter-of-factness and an originality of expression; like the beginning of *Pride and Prejudice* it lends itself to being memorized and, as with Austen's commencement, the reader may suspect an authorial intent, a voice lurking behind the apparently straightforward statement. Such a suspicion is strengthened by the quotation from the Latin Mass ('I will go in to the altar of God') that immediately follows the first paragraph and with the realization that the Catholic Mass and the epic invocation are being parodied the reader enters the mimetic and self-reflexive language world of *Ulysses*.

The first book of the *Odyssey* presents an unhappy young Telemachus who is unsettled, feeling dispossessed by the antics of usurping suitors who lounge insouciantly about his home waiting to see which of them will marry his mother. In *Ulysses* Stephen has returned from Paris for his mother's death, nearly a year earlier, but he also does not feel at home. The usurping suitor in the first book of *Ulysses* takes the form of the British presence and the cultural hegemony of the Anglo-Irish in Ireland. The antagonisms generated therein resonate in the relationships between Stephen, Mulligan and Haines.

Mulligan's complacent self-assurance and his unctuous proposals – to visit Athens (1.42–3), to Hellenise Ireland (1.158) – are experienced by Stephen as forms of enticement that trespass on his troubled mind. Mulligan feels too at home with his environment: he whistles once and waits in confident anticipation for the twin calls from the departing mailboat; he is cockily sure about handling Haines and nonchalant about acquiring the key for the tower. When Stephen informs Haines of his servitude, to the British state, to the Catholic Church and to a third unnamed master who sometimes calls upon his services (1.638–41), Mulligan and his class may be this third master. Earlier, when thinking of tidying up for Mulligan by carrying his shaving bowl, Stephen sees himself as his servant, albeit 'a servant of a servant' (1.312). Mulligan becomes a servile figure by playing at being Irish with his parodic, but nonetheless pandering, ethnographic chat to Haines of 'fishgods' in 'the year of the big wind' (1.367). At other times he drops easily into English public-school parlance – 'in a funk' (1.59), 'spiffing' (1.118), 'give him a ragging' (1.163) – and is willing to proffer Dedalus to Haines as an exemplar of native wit while at the same time, for the short-term gains it will bring, inveigling Stephen to work with and not against the Englishman.

The first book of the *Odyssey* ends with Telemachus contemplating departure and a solitary journey to find news of his father; Joyce's first chapter concludes with a like-minded resolution ('I will not sleep here tonight. Home also I cannot go.') and the final word, in response to Mulligan's voice calling to him from the sea, is 'Usurper'. The Homeric correspondences, however, are never mechanical or predictable and the social class difference between Stephen and Mulligan, felt by both of them and meticulously observed by Joyce, are part of a political dimension rooted in a non-Homeric, historically specific context. The resistance of Telemachus to the suitors morphs into the struggle of a young Irish intellectual against the disempowering influence of English power and the self-interested willingness of Mulligan's class to compromise with those who rule. Haines is enlightened and progressive in some respects – he is learning some Gaelic and half-apologizes for English misrule (1.648) – but his imperial and racist identity is stressed by Joyce: he is 'the seas' ruler' (1.574), his family's wealth comes from colonial interests in South Africa (1.156) and he is anti-semitic (1.667).

Issues of servitude crystallize around the old milkwoman and her role in this chapter shows Joyce's adroit use of links with the *Odyssey*. In the Greek epic, Telemachus is visited by the goddess Athena in disguise and chided by him for not confronting the suitors. Athena tells Telemachus that his father is not dead and that he should journey away from home to seek news of Odysseus. The milkwoman is described (1.404–5) as a disguised immortal 'serving her conqueror [Haines] and her gay betrayer [Mulligan]' but she also represents a servile Ireland (silk of the kine and poor old woman were commonly used epithets for the country) and Stephen is unsure what message she brings for him. He objects to the way she accepts the authority of someone like Mulligan, certain only of the worth of his own insubordination and his steadfast spirit of revolt. When Mulligan ingratiatingly takes his arm (1.159) the passage of realist dialogue is interrupted by four words referring to a Cranly and the reader is unexpectedly sharing Stephen's memory of a friend who tried to convince him not to abandon the Church. The reader needs to have read *A Portrait of an Artist as a Young Man* to know who Cranly is and why, towards the end of that novel, Stephen rejected the comforting theology that Cranly offered. Such knowledge adds to an understanding of why Stephen rejects the acquiescence that Mulligan represents.

In his deracinated loneliness, Stephen is a Hamlet-like figure and there are enough references to Shakespeare's play in this chapter to make the comparison a convincing one. Mulligan is akin to the usurper Claudius, not least when he upbraids Stephen for mourning excessively (though it is the ghost of his mother, not his father, who haunts Stephen's consciousness), and like Hamlet Stephen is tortured with the self-awareness of his angst. The sense that the reader shares Stephen's inner thoughts would seem to confirm the conventional nature of the chapter's narrative style but there are moments that disturb the narrative flow and help prepare the reader for what is to come later in the novel. When Mulligan is being cajolingly intimate with Stephen by assuring him that Haines can be dealt with, there follows a passage describing the 'ragging' of an Oxford student and how, outside on the quadrangle, a 'deaf gardener, aproned, masked with Matthew Arnold's face, pushes his mower on the sombre lawn' (1.172–5). The meaning of this reference is not provided for within the text and no interpretation is offered. Is this the interior voice of Stephen, part of a stream of consciousness guaranteeing his subjectivity, or a textual supplement or intrusion commenting on Stephen's plight? As with Hamlet, Stephen is in search of his identity but hostile to those being proffered to him. Arnold's *Culture and Anarchy* (1869) envisaged a blend of Hebraic and Hellenic impulses producing a new cultural temperament of 'sweetness and light' but any such liberal vision is rejected by Stephen. The unedifying spectacle of gardener Arnold serenely deaf to the violence occurring around him points to Stephen's quarrel with Britain's Victorian liberalism.

A different kind of fluctuation in the narrative style of this chapter comes with the sense that Joyce might be playing with the linguistic norms governing the conventional narrative voice. A sentence like 'He [Mulligan] shaved evenly and with care, in silence, seriously' (1.99) seems unnecessarily fastidious and, taking just the first page as an example, there is a surfeit of adverbs: 'he said sternly . . . he cried briskly . . . he said gaily'. This may reflect the role-playing nature of Mulligan but its 'unmistakeable ring of Edwardian novelese'[1] also suggests a mild parody on Joyce's part of the cliché-prone idiom of conventional fiction, a mimicking of a certain way of writing.[2]

NESTOR

Time

9–10 a.m.

Place

Mr Deasy's school in Dalkey Avenue, Dalkey, one mile south of Sandycove.

Plot

Stephen Dedalus is teaching a class prior to a morning break that heralds a hockey game. It is a half-day for the school and Stephen's payday. Deasy gives Stephen a letter about foot and mouth disease, hoping to see it published in a newspaper.

Stephen conducts a class in history and English (with some extra coaching in maths for one pupil) before collecting his salary and listening to the well-intentioned but patronizing Deasy deliver misogynistic and anti-semitic pronouncements on history.

Discussion

In the *Odyssey*, Telemachus leaves his home in Ithaca and travels first to the palace of Nestor at Pylos for news of his father. The elderly Nestor receives him well and relates what he knows about the fate of Greeks on their way home from Troy before advising Telemachus to visit Menelaus in Sparta for information about Odysseus. This episode becomes for Joyce a peg on which to hang a short narrative, with Nestor transformed into Mr Deasy; its aim to question the nature of history and the mindset of moderate Unionism in particular. More general epistemological doubts move like an unsettling current through this chapter.

British Prime Minister Gladstone became converted to the policy of home rule for Ireland and introduced a bill to this effect in 1886 but it failed to gain the full support of the Liberal Party that he headed and was defeated in the Commons. The bill did not cater for the interests of Ulster Protestants and their political opposition to home rule found cultural expression in a discourse of difference that stressed the Englishness of Ulster loyalists as opposed to the Celtic nature of the Irish.[3] This discourse is reflected in Deasy's distancing of himself from the unworldly (2.236–7) and error-prone (2.270–2) Catholic Irish and his self-promotion as a man of efficient industriousness (2.331, 420) and sound good sense (2.229–30). Stephen resists Deasy's voluble dogmatism and occlusions, remembering the Protestant pogroms (2.273–6), and offers an overt quietism to his bigotry (2.345–377). Ironically, and fatally undermining his show of worldly wisdom, Deasy's pronouncements on history are mostly muddled and misinformed and reveal some of the very qualities that he thinks his superior Ulster identity rises above.[4] The chapter ends with an emphatic display of his anti-semitism and his ignorance (contrary to what he says (2.442), a Jewish community had been in Dublin for three centuries) and, as with Telemachus after his visit to Nestor, Stephen has learnt little of what he wants to know (2.404).

Underlying the discourse of difference there is, in terms that might gain Deasy's approval, a contrast between authoritative knowledge and a feckless waywardness. Deasy takes control in his role as a teacher (2.191) while Stephen exhibits a laxness (2.29); Deasy is certain about his grasp on facts (2.390–6) whereas Stephen sees himself as open only to the possibility of acquiring knowledge (2.403). The underlying disparity in their epistemologies – a concern that goes beyond differences in their respective characters as individuals – accounts for the gap that is opened up between an objective catechism of historical 'facts' (2.1–5) and the likelihood that what is recorded as history is subjectively 'fabled by the daughters of memory' (2.7). The past happens but what is recorded for posterity is not necessarily the whole picture –'and yet it was in some way if not as memory fabled it' (2.7) – and while history records an old woman ('a bedlam') stunning Pyrrhus with a roof-tile (2.48) what is not registered is what might have happened had the roof-tile missed him. History has 'branded' and 'fettered' what is 'lodged in the room of the infinite possibilities they have ousted' (2.50) and this invites metaphysical speculation (2.51–2). It also provokes Stephen into thinking about how what has taken place, history, has ossified the unequal relationship between England and Ireland (2.42–7). Stephen, thinking how his imaginative definition of a pier would delight Haines, considers the role of 'court jester to the English'[5] that becomes his possible destiny and he wonders why some Irish accept such a role. 'Not wholly for the smooth caress' (2.45) is an indication of hesitancy about the certainty of his knowledge and the 'Nestor' chapter as a whole is very much about doubting; for some critics, the uncertainty of knowledge extends to the authority of meaning that language seems to possess.

Doubt about how language works is one way of trying to make sense of Stephen's riddle (2.102–7), the answer to which (2.115) proves as inexplicable to readers of *Ulysses* as it does to the pupils in his class. If history and the strait-jacketing of its possibilities are interrogated in the 'Nestor' chapter, how is Joyce to express this and undermine existing categories of ordering events without falling into the trap of repeating terms of fixity in his own writing? Partly by taking on board Deasy's discourse of difference and running it to ground by decentring the signifiers that for some endow history with coherence and stability; hence a riddle that cannot be unriddled, the posing of a question that cannot be decoded to produce a satisfactory answer. Hélène Cixous puts it neatly when, introducing Stephen's riddle as an example of Joyce's strategy of hesitancy, she compares the effect to that of thinking we hear a key turning in a door only to realize there is no door and what gave the notion credence was only the sound of a key.[6] The posing of a riddle places Stephen in Deasy's role as a holder of knowledge, provider of the sense that will put the riddle right, but the answer he provides – the fox burying his grandmother under a hollybush– is as enigmatic as the original puzzle; it remains undecipherable and, as such, destabilizes its own mastery because it only provides the knowledge of non-knowledge.[7]

PROTEUS

Time

11 a.m.

Place

Sandymount Strand, further up the coast from Dalkey and beyond Sandycove, in the direction of central Dublin.

Plot

An introspective Stephen walks along the strand, meditating on space and phenomena and thinking of calling on his uncle and aunt. His time in Paris is recalled with self-mockery and he remembers an Irish political rebel he met there. Stephen encounters a dog and the people with it; thoughts of death disturb his mind. He looks back and sees a three-master moving silently through the water towards Dublin.

Discussion

The exact route of Stephen's physical journey from the Dalkey school to the strand at Sandymount is not determinable and while there is consensus that he must have taken a train from Dalkey, and not walked the nine miles to the strand, there is disagreement about where he got off the train and at what time he was actually walking along the strand.[8] The text says nothing about the route taken but this has not stopped some Joycean scholars from pondering the different ways he might have travelled, as if a journey from the school to the strand really did occur on 16 June 1904. Such possibilities, the might-have-happened moments that are always present, occupy some of Stephen's metaphysical musings on the strand and as such they continue, in a way, the thoughts about history that opened the 'Nestor' chapter. The difference is that 'Proteus' is a far more forbidding chapter and this is related to how interior monologue, noticeable in short pulses in 'Telemachus' and increasingly apparent in 'Nestor', now constitutes the whole. Not a word is spoken in this stream of consciousness chapter that charts the quickly changing thoughts and sensations in the mind of an incredibly erudite young man; the intense interiority of this chapter makes it difficult for the eavesdropping reader to follow the condensed flow of language.

The Homeric parallel concerns the visit of Telemachus to the court of Menelaus, someone who knows of Odysseus' lot from information coerced out of the shape-changing sea god Proteus. The sea god's knowledge that Odysseus is marooned on Calypso's island is obtained with difficulty by Menelaus because of Proteus' ability to change his appearance and elude capture; by way of a very general correspondence, Stephen in this chapter also grapples with the nature of change over space ('the modality of the visible'). What presents a challenge for the reader is that any cognitive mapping of 'Proteus' has to follow the chapter's own protean nature: rapid changes of thought that flow from one prose movement to another ensure that the medium is the message in this fusion of form and content. The reader has to hold on to the shifting language just as Menelaus had to wrestle with Proteus changing shape.

To get started, the following breakdown by line numbers may help in getting a grip on the chapter's movement and the dense knots of literary, linguistic, ecclesiastical, philosophical and historical references.

3.1–9: abstract thoughts on the nature of the visible, via the reflections of Aristotle, whom Dante called the master of those who know ('*maestro di color che sanno*'), through colours and, before that, material objects (ineluctable means inescapable and diaphane means transparent).

10–24: thoughts on the audible as Stephen closes his eyes; 'Nacheinander' refers here to the way things succeed each other in time, and 'Nebeneinander' the way they are beside each other in space; the origin of rhythm in patterns of sounds heard aloud.

29–40: two women follow behind him on the strand. Taking them to be midwives, Stephen imagines a network of navels connecting everyone back to Eve and a telephone call made to Eden.

45–54: thoughts on his own birth and the sexual act that made it possible; the father–son relationship brings to mind Arius, a priest from the fourth century who maintained that the Son of God was not consubstantial with God the Father, and Stephen coins the unwieldy 'constransmagnificandjewbangtantiality' (incorporating 'consubstantiality', 'transubstantiality', 'magnificat/magnificent', 'Jew', and 'bang') to describe the controversies that Arius stirred up.

58–103: after recalling the arrangement to meet Mulligan at midday, he thinks of calling on his aunt and uncle and their son (Sarah, Richie and Walter) who live nearby and imagines how his visit would proceed (his father's snobbish ridicule of his brother-in-law affects Stephen's recreation of the scene).

105–119: an especially dense paragraph moving with speed from thoughts of his family's social status, to the library near St Patrick's cathedral where Jonathan Swift was dean and then to a description of a strange church event.

120–7: thoughts of the Eucharist and Occam the fourteenth-century logician and friar.

161–2: Looking towards Dublin's electric power station, the Pigeonhouse, thoughts of blasphemous lines from Leo Taxil's *La Vie de Jesus* (Paris, 1884). Joseph asks the pregnant Mary who has put her in this 'fichue position' ('deplorable situation'); she answers that it was the pigeon (dove, symbol of the Holy Ghost). Issues of paternity, as in 2.45–54 above.

163–8: First recall of Kevin Egan and his son Patrice; based on a Fenian in exile that Joyce met in Paris in 1903.

74–199: various reflections on his time in Paris, arriving there too late to catch a post office open to cash his money order and departing prematurely when his father telegrams news of his mother's death (a printing error on the actual telegram Joyce received spelt 'mother' as 'nother').

216–44: recall of time in a café in Paris with Kevin Egan, a fictional character based on a Fenian who was imprisoned in a London jail (Clerkenwell) and whose attempted rescue by comrades using gunpowder failed and led to the death of bystanders. A minor language problem with the waitress overcome, they talk of Ireland and her revolutionaries, their plots and disguises.

245–264: more memories of Egan, sought out by Stephen in the three taverns that the sad exile moves between. His wife is indifferent towards him and his deeds are forgotten: 'loveless, landless, wifeless'.

300–9: Viking invaders landed on the beach and his ancestors came there to hack meat off a dead whale; sharing of a blood-inheritance with 'my people'.

310–30: the dog, belonging to the cocklepickers, that he spotted earlier (2.294) runs towards him barking; thoughts of pretenders who claimed the throne and how Mulligan saved a man from drowning while he himself is scared by a dog. He thinks of the drowned man whose body has yet to be found (mentioned earlier, 1.672–7).

342–64: the dog, Tatters, becomes Proteus as he changes into a bear (2.345), a wolf (2.346), calf (2.348), fox (2.361) and panther (2.363).

365–9: thought of a panther brings Haines's dream (1.57) to mind and then his own dream from which Haines awoke him; a dream of the Orient and an inviting man with a melon.

370–98: the cocklepickers are identified by Stephen as gypsies and their lingo feeds the lines of verse that come to him; he thinks of a gypsy woman he saw as a prostitute. The cocklepickers pass him by, noticing his hat, and Stephen composes to himself new lines of verse that become erotic in nature.

401–7: Stephen plays with the sounds of words and tears off the bottom of Deasy's letter so as to be able to jot down his poetry.

408–23: return to metaphysical musings on space and time and, via Berkeley ('the good bishop of Cloyne'), the idea that what is taken for reality is more like a screen, a veil, to be read for its signs rather than experienced through sight as something real. He studies his own act of seeing.

424–36: thoughts of an ideal woman turn to a real one seen on the street a few days earlier.

453–69: Stephen, relieving himself, watches his water flow around him; composes an onomatopoeic 'wavespeech' to represent the hissing sounds of waves on the sand and, with an excess of alliteration, the running water becomes its own stream of phonemes.

470–81: he remembers the drowned man (1.673–5); pictures the recovery of the body and considers a sea-change cycle that brings home the disturbing proximity to death in our daily lives: 'Dead breaths I living breathe, tread dead dust, devour a urinous offal from all dead.'

489–502: after noticing clouds in the sky, he picks up his stick; an array of disparate thoughts fill his mind. He looks for the hand-kerchief that Mulligan used (1.69), picks his nose and senses there might be someone there behind him.

503–5: looking back, he sees a ship moving towards Dublin port and its masts, hauled up to rest on cross-timbers, resembling three crosses on the horizon. This memorable description evokes for some a religious symbol, to others a homecoming, something that is due. These portentous three lines share with the last sentence of the 'Nestor' chapter a lyricism that is at odds with the lines that come before them.

The above notes are by no means comprehensive and this chapter, more than most, benefits from being read with the help of annotations (see pages 114–5); as more references are unravelled the text of 'Proteus' becomes less impenetrable, though negotiating the intertextual density takes time and patience. It is easy to falter, feeling it is a Pyrrhic success of sorts – 'another victory [chapter] like that and we are done for' (2.14) – but the reader should take heart from the suggestion of serenity in that final image of the three-master sailing into the Dublin docks. The tone is quite different to the sense of instability, flux and anxiety that has characterized Stephen for much of the book's first three chapters. Stephen, pressed on by the 'nightmare' (2.377) of his country's history, finds his thoughts polarized and this robs him of equilibrium. Joyce, speaking of Stephen in these chapters, admitted: 'I haven't let this young man off very lightly' and also saw how 'he has a shape that can't be changed.'[9] Change will come but from a different sort of person – an Irish Jew – and to see how this is the case the narrative returns the reader to 8 o'clock in the morning but this time to a different location.

CALYPSO

Time

8–8.45 a.m.

Place

Bloom's house, 7 Eccles Street, north of Dublin's River Liffey.

Plot

Leopold Bloom, 38 years old and an advertisement canvasser, is preparing breakfast and makes a short journey to a butcher's shop to buy a pork kidney. Back home, three items of mail are waiting: a card and letter from his daughter Milly and a letter for his wife, Molly. He takes the mail up to the bedroom with Molly's breakfast and she tells him that the letter is from Blazes Boylan who will be calling in the afternoon, ostensibly to deliver a programme for the concerts in which Molly is singing. He hurries down to the kitchen, where his kidney is burning, and after breakfast he visits the outdoor toilet and brings a copy of *Titbits* to read and use as toilet paper. He is dressed in black for an acquaintance, Paddy Dignam, whose funeral he will be attending later in the morning. Dignam comes to mind as he hears a local church bell ringing at 8.45.

Discussion

In Book 5 of the *Odyssey* Odysseus is on the island of the nymph Calypso, held captive there for seven years, but on the verge of being released after Athena's successful intervention with Zeus on his behalf. Other than to see Bloom as Odysseus, Homeric correspondences with this chapter of Joyce's novel are not obvious or enlightening. There is a painted nymph over the bed (4.369) but as Molly is the faithful Penelope of Homer's tale (though planning adultery with Boylan) it is not clear who might be a Calypso figure. In what way, too, is Bloom a prisoner, or an exile in thrall to a nymph? His identity as a Jew is one way of situating Bloom's difference from the society in which he dwells. On his walk to the butcher's shop, he daydreams yearningly about the Orient (4.84–98) and in the shop he picks up a sheet of paper for wrapping meat and sees an advertisement there for a settlement in Palestine. Bloom realizes Dlugacz the butcher is a Zionist – 'I thought he was' (4.156) – and he fondly imagines a settlement in Palestine. Jewishness, though, is an identity he cannot fully embrace and as a cloud covers the sun the Palestinian landscape becomes a horrid and sterile one. An old woman crossing the street (evocative herself of the milkwoman in 'Telemachus') evokes for Bloom the plight of Jews wandering the world and this identification effects a symbiosis of sorts between the Irish and Jews. This in a way is Bloom's plight and though he thinks of himself as Irish he is also Jewish; the result is that he is not fully at home in either race. Nor is he at home in his own house, as the letter waiting on the hall floor soon makes clear to him. What emerges from the 'Calypso' chapter is the way Bloom's divided and alienated self is positioned and articulated within terms of an Irish–Jewish identification. The analogy between the two races was first raised in 'Proteus' when Kevin Egan is mourned as a forgotten hero in Paris in a phrase associated with the Jews in captivity (Psalms 137: 1–2): 'They have forgotten Kevin Egan, not he them. Remembering thee, O Sion' (4.263).

Bloom's sense of desolation is overcome by his striving to think ahead and imagine the simple pleasures of a breakfast and proximity to a bed-warmed Molly (4.233–42). His elected affinities are physical and sensual in a way that differentiates him from Stephen: instead of the young aesthete's self-disgust at eating 'urinous offal' (3.479) Bloom enjoys 'the inner organs of beasts and fowls' (4.1) and so different is his take on the world that the 'Calypso' chapter reads like a fresh beginning to the novel. Yet there are parallels with Stephen: both are dressed in mourning black, both are without their door keys and the cloud that covers the sun at 4.218 is described in the same terms as the one at 1.248 (where for Stephen it also prefaces a spell of depression). Bloom's 15-year-old daughter, Milly, who is away from home in Mullingar apprenticed to a photographer is the girl spoken about in Stephen's presence in the first chapter (1.684).

'Calypso' is an easy chapter to read, with a strong third-person narrator alternating with passages of Bloom's often mundane and fleeting thoughts; his earthy consciousness contrasts with Stephen's abstruse intellectualizing and is more accessible to the reader. Some details surface that are not immediately explained. When he first leaves his house Bloom looks inside his hat (4.70) for the white slip of paper with his name and he checks too for a potato that he likes to carry as a talisman. The context in which a Rudy (4.419) is mentioned suggests there was a son who died after childbirth. The first of these moments is soon returned to in the next chapter.

LOTUS EATERS

Time

9.30–10.30 a.m.

Place

Sir John Rogerson's Quay on the south bank of the Liffey (Bloom has walked there from his home, over a mile away, around the time Stephen was walking the same distance to the school at Dalkey), streets to the south towards the Westland Row post office and then a little way further south to a public bathhouse.

Plot

Using a *nom de plume*, Bloom collects a letter from a post office and having just opened it he is interrupted by an acquaintance, C. P. M'Coy. Eventually alone, he reads a coy reply from a Martha Clifford (possibly the letter-writer's own pseudonym), a woman with whom he is carrying on an epistolary affair. He then enters a nearby church, observing the Mass in progress, before leaving to walk on to a chemist's shop to order a skin lotion for his wife. Another acquaintance accosts him on the street, Bantam Lyons, who is interested in the runners for that day's Ascot Gold Cup. When Bloom offers him his newspaper, saying he was going to throw it away, Bantam Lyons takes this as a tip (Throwaway is a runner in the race). Unaware, Bloom then walks on to a bathhouse prior to his attendance at Dignam's funeral.

Discussion

An awareness of the Homeric correspondence – the visit of Odysseus and his crew to an island of lotus eaters in order to collect water – provides a useful way into this chapter. Three men of Odysseus's advance party meet the friendly inhabitants of the island and are offered the fruit of the flowering lotus plant to eat. The fruit induces a profound stupor and forgetfulness of home; only by forcing them back on to the ship and sailing away quickly is Odysseus able to prevent the rest of his crew from being infected with the same malaise.[10] In Joyce's chapter, the thoughts and experiences of Bloom evoke the Lotus Eaters in various ways but, Odysseus-like, he is able to deal with the predicament and carry on with his journey.

An early correspondence comes when Bloom conjures up images of oriental lethargy when looking in a shop window at packets of tea (5.29–34), and further parallels follow: in the post office, gazing at a British army recruitment poster, the depicted soldiers look hypnotized (5.65–74); the feeding horses seem stupefied (5.213–220) and, in what is a comical riff on this theme, the communicants in the church are victims of the opium of religion to the anthropologically minded Bloom (5.340–368). Bantam Lyons is addicted to gambling and C. P. M'Coy is under the delusion that he can once again cadge a suitcase (5.149 and 5.178–82).

'Lotus Eaters' is a chapter filled in a humorous spirit with reminders of how the self can surrender to attractive temptations and Bloom himself has to contend with sensual inducements that come his way. He struggles to maintain a conversation with M'Coy while watching a woman board a carriage across the street in the hope of catching a glimpse of her bare skin and the chapter ends with his vision of an indolent sojourn in the bath.

Bloom's route can be plotted accurately on a street map of Dublin – just as Joyce would have done when composing his character's perambulation – and it reveals a topographical aspect that is worth noting He does not take a direct route to the post office but circles his way towards it and while on the one hand this accords with the surreptitious nature of his journey it also reflects the lotus-eating-induced languidness which seeps through this episode like the imagined release of beer from the barrels: 'a huge dull flood leaked out, flowing together, winding through mudflats all over the level land, a lazy pooling swirl of liquor bearing along wideleaved flowers of its froth' (5.315–7). This sentence appears when Bloom is standing under a railway arch and tearing into pieces the envelope of Martha Clifford's letter. He thinks how a valuable cheque could be similarly shredded and then about how much money is made from selling alcohol (which joins opium, tobacco, oats and communion wafers in a list of the chapter's plant-based narcotics). A clanking train passes overhead and the idea that the coaches carry beer barrels leads into the quoted sentence.

The question arises: whose voice is at work here? The paragraph before ('What am I saying barrels? Gallons. About a million barrels all the same.') is clearly a part of Bloom's interior monologue and the paragraph that follows ('He had reached the open backdoor of All Hallows.') equally clearly belongs to a third-person narrative. This objective narrative voice begins the paragraph in question ('An incoming train . . .') but the image of beer lazily flooding the land seems to occupy a space somewhere between the two; while it possibly emerges out of the character's mind the language is not Bloom's and the 'wideleaved flowers' of froth trope is part of the floral motif that runs through this chapter.[11]

It is significant for what will become an increasingly pronounced feature of *Ulysses* – what might be called language for language's sake – is the way this chapter's Homeric analogue initially invites a particular theme, in this case the druggy lotus plant, only to see it amplified in ways that take the reader beyond the conventional narrative and traditional characterization of the novel form. It was a process that developed over time on the part of Joyce; something very apparent when the first appearance of this chapter (in July 1918 in the *Little Review*) is compared with its final form when the novel was published as a whole three years later. As Joyce revised the chapter in 1920–1 he intensified the floral motif so that, for example, with the passage describing Bloom's second reading of Martha's letter (5.260–7) he peppered it with the names of various flowers. Moments of linguistic bravado like the one just referred to are still just this – moments that interrupt the narrative flow – and the reader, anyway, is likely to remain more engaged with the character of Bloom. He thinks of his father when seeing an advertisement for a performance of *Leah* and his father's alienated plight as an immigrant Jew touches Bloom's memory (5.194–209).

A final chronological note to this chapter. When Bloom leaves the church he notes the time as 10.15 (5.462) and, taking into account the visit to the chemist's shop and meeting with Bantam Lyons, it is around 10.30 when he enters the bathhouse. He needs to reach Dignam's house around 11a.m. for the start of the funeral procession and as this requires a ten-minute tram journey his bath is not the leisurely affair that the chapter's final paragraph envisages. This, perhaps, is why his anticipated masturbation (5.503–5) does not occur; Odysseus-like, our hero Bloom must hurry away from the land of lotus eaters and continue on his journey.

HADES

Time

11a.m.–12 noon

Place

From Sandymount, across the city centre, to Glasnevin Cemetery in the north of Dublin

Plot

Bloom joins three acquaintances in a carriage for a funeral procession from the house of Paddy Dignam in Sandymount, south Dublin, to the cemetery on the other side of the city.

Discussion

This chapter's Homeric analogue, the journey of Odysseus to Hades, the underworld, in the hope of finding news about his home, works at a structural level – Bloom's journey to a cemetery for a funeral – and a thematic one – reflections on death and loss permeate this chapter – and this helps make the 'Hades' episode especially cohesive and focused. In one way it parallels the 'Proteus' chapter, this time as a window into the mind and heart of Bloom, though it is a far easier and more enjoyable chapter to read than 'Proteus'.

Bloom is seen in a social situation with fellow Dubliners but he is not accepted as an equal (they are on first-name terms with one another but he is called by his surname) and remains on the periphery of their circle. Discombobulated by the anti-semitic sentiments of his fellow travellers, he fails in his attempt to tell a funny story about the Jew Reuben J. Dodd (6.251–91). Feelings of loss inhabit Bloom's consciousness – for his child Rudy, who died a few weeks after birth, and for the silent suffering that lay behind his father's suicide – in ways that are not made available for his companions in the funeral carriage. Bloom is able to extend his sympathies to all those affected by death though he remains undeceived, acknowledging the finality of death and able to laugh at the irrelevance of

Christian theology. He accepts death and bodily dissolution without undue trepidation and, like the fearless Odysseus, returns intact from his visit to the underworld. The snub he receives from the haughty Menton, who bears a grudge against him over a game of bowls, cannot harm the sanguine Bloom.

Having reached the end of the novel's first six chapters, it is a good time to take stock and look back at what has been read. Unless the reader has had time to work through some of the numerous allusions and references in the text there will be much in the way of detail that has been passed over but hopefully this does not prove an insuperable barrier to following the narrative, relating to the characters and enjoying the text. While Stephen's intellectualism is forbidding at times his angst is not and his troubled relationship with Mulligan remains unresolved – will he hold to the agreement (1.733–4) that they meet in The Ship pub at 12.30? The degree of intersubjectivity between reader and character is increased with the more engaging Bloom and he endears himself to many readers by way of his compassion, curiosity and humanism; and the uncertainty surrounding his relationship with his wife Molly. The stream of consciousness technique has been employed in all six chapters and there is a discernible third-person voice guiding the narrative. As has been noted, however, there are places where the language seems to become disengaged from the demands of the story, drawing attention to itself at a variety of levels: single words, like the spellings of the cat's miaows with a silent 'g' on the first page of 'Calypso', reminding the reader of words like 'gnaw' and 'gnome'; sentences such as the exquisitely crafted one that brings 'Proteus' to an end; or a thematic motif like the use of floral language in 'Lotus Eaters'. There is also a sense emerging of the interlinking of episodes, both in chronological ways (like the same cloud covering the sun in 'Telemachus' and 'Calypso') and by way of a broader awareness that Stephen, the Telemachus figure in search of a father, and Bloom, who has lost his son, may be destined to meet. In 'Hades' their paths do cross for the first time when Bloom sees Stephen at Sandymount from the window of his carriage – giving substance to the possibility that Stephen's dream recalled earlier in 'Proteus' (3.365–9) prefigures the helping hand that Bloom will later extend to him.

The textual richness of *Ulysses* is a goldmine for literary critics who discern patterns and themes of varying complexity and an example in terms of the first six chapters may be taken from the work of Richard Ellmann. He detects a triadic organization to Joyce's novel – a reasonable thesis so far given that the first three chapters concern Stephen and the following three Bloom – and the influence of the theories of Giambattista Vico who postulated a cycle of theocratic, aristocratic and democratic ages that repeated itself in a progressive manner. Hence:

> The first chapter begins with a mass and ends with a priest, and its equivalent in Bloom's experience, the fourth, begins with the steeple of George's church and ends with its 'high up' bells. The second and fifth chapters play different variations on the theme of aristocracy, as Stephen teaches at a rich boys' school and listens to the headmaster discourse of princes and kings' sons, and as Bloom ogles an aristocratic lady about to get up into her carriage, then ponders on the ways of the Anglo-Irish Trinity College and the Kildare street club. In the third and sixth chapters both Stephen and Bloom take a more democratic view; Stephen utters good doctrine when he says, 'You will not be masters of others or their slave', and Bloom finds an apt parable in the democracy of death. Seen in this Vichian light, the sudden appearance of the ship *Rosavean* at the end of *Proteus* heralds a change, a *ricorso*, a reformulation of Stephen's state. At the end of *Hades*, Bloom emerges from the Stygian darkness to ascend through the gates to a kind of new birth, which is substantiated by the imagery of *starting* and of *delivery* at the beginning of the seventh chapter.[12]

It is certainly true that Joyce knew about Vico's theories but whether or not he consciously configured the pattern outlined above and whether this provides a helpful insight into the first six chapters is less definite.

AEOLUS

Time

12 noon

Place

Offices of the *Freeman's Journal* and *Evening Telegraph* in the centre of Dublin.

Plot

Bloom, working to secure a graphic advertisement for a grocer named Alexander Keyes, obtains a previous copy of a Keyes advertisement and takes it to the head printer, Nannetti. The printer accepts the proposed modification but stipulates that the advertisement should run for three months. Bloom decides to telephone Keyes to confirm his agreement and encounters in the office Simon Dedalus, Ned Lambert and a Professor MacHugh. An unemployed barrister, J. J. O'Molloy, the editor Myles Crawford and Lenehan, a sports journalist, join them. Before long, Lambert and Dedalus leave for a pub and, after his phone call, Bloom leaves to catch Keyes who is in a nearby auction room. Stephen Dedalus arrives, with Deasy's letter about foot and mouth disease, accompanied by Mr O'Madden Burke. There ensues a conversation about oratory, followed by a mass exit to the pub; in the street outside Bloom reappears and seeks the editor's agreement about renewing the advertisement for only two months.

Discussion

The Homeric correspondence, the visit of Odysseus and his crew to the island of Aeolia, provides Joyce with a platform for this chapter's foray into the windy language of rhetoric and journalism. On the island Odysseus is helped by Aeolus who gives him a bag which confines the winds (except for the one that would bear the Greeks home) but the crew, thinking there is gold in the bag, later open it and the released winds drive them all back to the island. Joyce takes a figurative use of windy – inflated or bombastic talk, high-sounding but empty language – and applies it in a variety of ways throughout this chapter.

The most noticeable application appears in the rhetorical cross-heads that punctuate the text. These headline-style titles were added by Joyce when reworking the chapter in 1921 and while they appear appropriate in so far as the setting is a newspaper office they are also interruptive and intrusive; the overall intent seems to be a whimsical conflation of form and content. The headlines are anonymous, not predicated on a single consciousness, reminding us of printing rather than an authorial voice and ranging from the banal ('SHORT BUT TO THE POINT.') to a humorous mixing of the literary and the populist ('SOPHIST WALLOPS HAUGHTY HELEN SQUARE ON PROBOSCIS, SPARTANS GNASH MOLARS. ITHACANS VOW PEN IS CHAMP.'). They become progressively more trivial, losing whatever political edge some of the earlier ones possessed ('THE WEARER OF THE CROWN'), as if charting a decline in the meaningful use of language or just enjoying the burlesque.

A less noticeable displacement effect whereby the writing wilfully draws attention to itself is found in the employment of rhetorical tropes, used in the first version of this chapter that appeared in *The Little Review* in October 1918 but much supplemented by Joyce when adding to the galley proofs three years later. Most of these rhetorical devices are not obvious to the reader but some, like the first sentence of the 'GENTLEMEN OF THE PRESS' sequence, insist on being noticed.[13] The sentence in question originally appeared twice as a straightforward instance of the rhetorical device of repetition but in 1921 Joyce incorporated this effect into the more sophisticated grammatical figure of chiasmus (inverting the order of words in two parallel clauses): 'Grossbooted draymen rolled barrels dullthudding out of Prince's stores and bumped them up on the brewery float. On the brewery float bumped dullthudding barrels rolled by grossbooted draymen out of Prince's stores.' (7.21–24) In the act of reading it is not necessary to identify this as an example of chiasmus in order to sense that the syntax is on display here, at play with itself, and this is part of the chapter's larger concern with the way language works. Just as Bloom is concerned to make the Keyes advertisement communicate effectively, the characters in the newspaper office discuss what makes for good oratory and journalism; the chapter as a whole seems more concerned with how language operates than with the interior thoughts of its characters. There is an interesting example of this when someone lights J. J. O'Molloy's cigar and we read: 'I have often thought since on looking back over that strange time that it was that small act, trivial in itself, that striking of that match, that determined the whole aftercourse of both our lives.' (7.763–5). Regardless of whether or not this is a thought belonging to Stephen – it is not clear and perhaps is not intended to be – there is play here with a conventional moment of textual melodrama in nineteenth-century fiction and one wonders if the deliberately clumsy repetition of 'that' is part of such a gentle mockery. The remark is not relevant to the plot of *Ulysses* – Stephen's life is not affected by the striking of the match – but within the conventions of another kind of fiction it would carry a rhetorical force and in this sense it has a place in a chapter that Joyce devotes to the persuasive qualities of language.

The reader buffeted about by the chapter's style and multiple allusions, struggles to follow the narrative as various characters come and go, as if they themselves are blown in contrary directions, and none more so than Bloom himself who, Odysseus-like, has to contend with difficulties that would thwart his purpose: first, Nannetti's stipulation about a three month renewal of the ad; followed by the task of contacting Keyes to seek his agreement; then the failure to reach the editor when he tries to reach him by phone; and the final rebuff from Crawford when Bloom returns to the newspaper office and catches him leaving for the pub.

If the chapter has its own prevailing wind, it is one that carries the blight of failure and the paralysing allure of language. The men in the newspaper office, who have all known better times in their professional lives, belong to the Irish Catholic intelligentsia, part of the generation that had looked to Parnell for leadership and which suffered from the sense of failure that came with his downfall. It is within this historical context that some sense can be made of Stephen's tale about the women who climb Nelson's pillar (a monument to the British admiral that stood in Dublin's city centre).[14] The parable is in part an ironic rejoinder to the vision of Moses overlooking the Promised Land. The plight of Moses and the Jews subjected to Egyptian rule arises in the conversation about a speech by John F. Taylor and the recall of the speech by Professor MacHugh (7.823–70) is both an encomium to Taylor's oratory and a warning about the power of words. Moses shuts his ears to the rhetoric and eloquence of the Egyptian overlords seeking Jewish submission and MacHugh's earlier caution – 'We mustn't be led away by words, by sounds of words. We think of Rome, imperial, imperious, imperative (7.483–5) – is allied to his argument (7.489–95, 561–70) that the spiritual and linguistic superiority of Greece (and by implication the Irish) is dismally ineffective when challenged by the material might of Rome (suggesting Ireland's conquest by England). Crawford is hopelessly inaccurate when it comes to history but he acknowledges a sense of failure when seeing himself as 'the fat in the fire. We haven't got the chance of a snowball in hell' (7.481–2).

Fine words and eloquence, the chapter is at times saying, may be all well and good but ultimately unsuccessful if used as the only weapon against political power. If the power of language is only something to be enjoyed for its own sake, merely savoured in the nostalgic manner of those exchanging their memories and anecdotes in the newspaper office, then is the quality of their discerning appreciation any more worthy than the frothy blather of the Dan Dawson that they so enjoy ridiculing (7.239–330). In Trieste in 1907 Joyce concluded a lecture on the cultural history of Ireland by expressing a view not dissimilar to this. He quoted approvingly a remark by Oscar Wilde about the Irish being "'the greatest talkers since the days of the ancient Greeks'" before adding 'but, though the Irish are eloquent, a revolution is not made from human breath'.[15]

Revolutions are made by working people and part of the distinctiveness of the 'Aeolus' chapter is that it features the world of work. While the characters in the newspaper office huff and puff over the speeches and journalism of the past, breaking off only to visit a pub, the print workers of *The Freeman's Journal* are busily employed in producing newsprint. The noise of the machinery and the work of typesetters and others are diligently recorded by Joyce: doors creak, scissors are wielded, a boy rushes in with the post, 'machines clanked in threefour time. Thump, thump, thump' (7.101), 'Sllt' (7.174), packing paper litters the floor, galley pages are checked, typesetters distribute type in reverse order and delivery boys wait for their papers. Other workers are out on the street creating their own orchestra of noises: the shout of tramline destinations, the call of shoeblacks, postal workers flinging sacks of mail and brewery draymen delivering barrels of stout. Bloom too is working and it seems fitting that the reader also has to work hard to follow a chapter with a number of minor characters coming and going and the historically specific nature of much of what they say.

LESTRYGONIANS

Time

1 p.m.–2 p.m.

Place

Central Dublin: Bloom walks down Sackville Street (O'Connell Street), across O'Connell Bridge, up Westmoreland Street, past

Trinity College and into Grafton Street, Duke Street, across Dawson Street and into Molesworth Street and Kildare Street.

Plot

Bloom, walking towards O'Connell Bridge, is handed a flyer advertising a gospel meeting. He spots a sister of Stephen Dedalus and, crossing the bridge, stops to feed some gulls with purchased cakes. He meets an old friend, Mrs Breen, whose odd husband is seeking legal advice after receiving an anonymous postcard, and learns that a mutual acquaintance, Mrs Purefoy, is in hospital. His visit to the Burton restaurant is curtailed by the sight of its diners greedily devouring their lunch and, instead, he eats at nearby Davy Byrne's pub. An acquaintance of Bloom, Nosey Flynn, is in the pub and when Bloom visits the toilet three more people enter the pub: Paddy Leonard, Tom Rochford and Bantam Lyons. Bloom leaves and, walking towards the National Library to collect a Keyes advertisement, he helps a blind young person cross a street. Spotting Blazes Boylan coming towards him, Bloom changes direction and passes through the gate of National Museum.

Discussion

The Linati scheme gives the chapter's technique as 'peristaltic', a physiological term for the alimentary canal's rhythmic contractions in the passage and digestion of food, and the chapter's 'organ' as the oesophagus; translated into the literary by Joyce this describes writing which, more so perhaps than in any other chapter in the book, is immensely impressive and pleasing in its aesthetic demonstration of Joyce's claim that his novel is 'the epic of the human body' (see page 16); the result of especially assiduous writing if Budgen's famous account relating to the composition of two of its sentences is to be taken at face value:

'I have been working hard on it all day,' said Joyce.
   'Does that mean that you have written a great deal?' I said.
   'Two sentences,' said Joyce . . .
'What are the words?' I asked.
'I believe I told you,' said Joyce, 'that my book is a modern *Odyssey*. Every episode in it corresponds to an adventure of

Ulysses. I am now writing the *Lestrygonians* episode, which corresponds to an adventure of Ulysses with the cannibals. My hero is going to lunch. But there is a seduction motive in the *Odyssey*, the cannibal king's daughter. Seduction appears in my book as women's silk petticoats hanging in a shop window. The words through which I express the effect of it on my hungry hero are: "Perfume of embraces all him assailed. With hungered flesh obscurely, he mutely craved to adore." You can see for yourself in how many different ways they might be arranged.'[16]

The chapter's concern with food and digestion is all-pervasive and multi-faceted but never, as it were, over cooked. Sometimes it operates on a psychological level: Bloom's thoughts periodically feast on pleasant memories of Molly but at other times stave off the realization that the usurper Boylan will soon be arriving at his home. In the first paragraph, when Bloom passes Lemon's confectionary store, food raises the presence of the Catholic church and the British state: a member of the Catholic teaching brotherhood, the Christian Brothers, is buying sweets for a class and Bloom notes the shop's advertisement of its royal license. The evangelist flyer evokes in Bloom thoughts of how religion feeds off notions of martyrdom and blood sacrifice (Dowie, Torry and Alexander are names of contemporary revivalists) and when he sees an underfed sister of Stephen, one of a family of fifteen children, he situates her plight in the context of Catholicism's attitude to women.

The chapter's peristaltic rhythm is conducted by modifications in Bloom's physiology – and this includes the nature of his thoughts and feelings – which are linked to changes in the state of his stomach during the course of his walk. At first he is not himself hungry and can think of others' need for nourishment; his reflections are generally sanguine, even when it comes to the police force that endangered his physical safety when he allowed himself to be caught up in protests over the British imperialist Joseph Chamberlain receiving an honorary degree in Trinity College (8.419–40). A mood of depression overtakes him – 'Feel as if I had been eaten and spewed' (8.495) – and colours his view of the world (8.476–92) until he spots John Howard Parnell; the uncanny resemblance to his deceased brother, Charles Stewart, and his sorrowful appearance occasions Bloom's witty diagnosis: 'Eaten a bad egg. Poached eyes on ghost' (8.508). He sees the poet A. E. Russell talking to a woman and the locus of food again shapes his observations (8.533–50) until mixed emotions about life with Molly begin to afflict him. He considers buying her something when looking in the window of Brown Thomas and he thinks again of Boylan's visit (8.620–33); an empty stomach is aggravating carnal disquiet as he enters the Burton restaurant. His disgust at what he sees is rendered in a powerful passage (8.650–93) where the vocabulary of consumption – 'swilling, wolfing . . . gurgling . . . spitting . . . bolting' – and the male physicality of 'wiping wetted moustaches . . . booser's eyes . . . beery piss . . .' evokes an equal revulsion in the reader.

Odysseus was able to escape from the cannibals because he avoided anchoring his ship in the bay of their island; Bloom flees the restaurant to find refuge in the safer berth of Davy Byrne's pub where he can finally relax and enjoy the chaste pleasure of a cheese sandwich mollified by a glass of wine. Peristalsis restores his body's balance and, expressed in a passage of jubilatory, sensuous prose (8.897–916), he relaxes by remembering time spent with Molly at Howth. After he leaves the pub, his composure unsettled by the sight of Boylan coming towards him, the prose becomes agitated and, like his breathing, its pace quickens as he struggles to cope by pretending to be looking for something (8.1188–93).

SCYLLA AND CHARYBDIS

Time

2 p.m.

Place

An office in the National Library.

Plot

Stephen is in the company, at various times, of the poet A. E. (George Russell), the librarian Lyster, assistant librarian and essayist John Eglinton and the library's director, Mr Best. Stephen propounds his reading of Shakespeare, though A. E. leaves prematurely for an appointment. Mulligan, who received a telegram sent by Stephen to the pub where they were supposed to have met earlier, turns up and joins the group. Bloom visits the library, enquiring about a provincial newspaper of the previous year which contains the Keyes design he needs. As Stephen and Mulligan are about to leave the library, Bloom passes out between them.

Discussion

The chapter's Homeric correspondence refers to the perilous voyage of Ulysses between the twin dangers of the multi-headed monster Scylla and the whirlpool Charybdis. While a theme relating to the negotiation of contending forces suggests itself, it is not immediately obvious how such a motif substantially patterns the structure or the content of this chapter. A clear association only seems to emerge at the very end when Stephen is about to leave the library and, sensing someone behind him, stands apart from his companion Mulligan to let the person through. That person is Bloom; Mulligan makes a brief address, having seen him earlier in the National Museum, while Stephen's encounter with him is again an unspoken one. The moment seems pregnant with meaning, with the physical space that Bloom creates between them signalling the sundering of Stephen's relationship with Mulligan – 'Part. The moment is now. Where then?' (9.1199) – a separation first heralded in the 'Telemachus' chapter.

Although Bloom can be seen as a Ulysses figure as he sails out of the library between the two young men it is not clear what dangers he is avoiding; it is, moreover, just one moment in a chapter which barely features Bloom. The more central matter at hand concerns interpretations of Shakespeare and it becomes the locus for an opposition between Stephen and his literary company. Sorting out the sense and significance of a Scylla and a Charybdis in this debate is no easy matter and the Homeric connection yields more insight when the reader thinks in terms of various antagonisms at work in the chapter rather than one core polarity. It is possible, for instance, to prioritize issues of paternity and personal identity in terms of the troubled consciousness of the young artist Stephen. As a Lacanian subject he struggles to establish an imaginary, immutable self-identity; as when pondering the money he has borrowed and not repaid:

> Wait. Five months. Molecules all change. I am other I now. Other I got pound.
> Buzz. Buzz.

> But I, entelechy, form of forms, am I by memory because under
> everchanging forms.
> I that sinned and prayed and fasted.
> A child Conmee saved from pandies.
> I, I and I. I. (9.205–12)

Stephen's theory of Shakespeare can be seen as paralleling this need
by insisting on a fixed identity for the playwright, one that forbids
any notion of chance, and it is only with Stephen's laugh (9.1016) that
he liberates himself from the search for a father figure; Shakespeare
'is no longer the controlling subject measuring word against world
but becomes the fugitive subject articulated from character to
character'.[17] While critics have had a field day spinning different
accounts of what is going on in this chapter, the more convincing
analyses are those that embed themselves in the cultural and political
currents with which Joyce engaged. Thus Stephen's wilful response to
being left out of A. E.'s anthology of Irish verse, 'See this. Remember' (9.294), is better understood as a hostile response to the Irish
Literary Revival rather than a lost opportunity to find his identity.

Coming back to the chapter's central debate, the reader's task is to
maintain a hold on the course of Stephen's virtuoso performance as
he sets forth his reading of Shakespeare. Difficulties are posed by the
frequent literary allusions, especially Shakespearian ones, and the
pace of reading slows to the snail-like if they are all to be taken
on board; fortunately this is not necessary to follow the argument.
Stephen's theory of Shakespeare is also subject to various interruptions – for example, by the chatter when A. E. is leaving about
the evening's literary meeting to which Stephen remains uninvited
(9.269–344). Such is the coming and going of characters that Eglinton
is the only one who is present for all of Stephen's talk. Then there
are moments of Stephen's interiority that pepper his dialogue, such
as the afore-cited recall of the money lent to him by A. E., initially
expressed in Shakespearian language, followed by a self-interrogation
that recalls moments from earlier chapters (and *A Portrait of the
Artist as a Young Man*) before jokingly concluding with 'A. E. I. O. U.'
(9.192–213). At one stage (9.893–933) the narrative voice disappears
altogether and is replaced by the dramatic form with headings for
the speakers, one of which, 'Mageelinjohn', combines John Eglinton
with the real name of the assistant librarian, William Magee, and

this becomes the occasion for another joke when he echoes Juliet's question to Romeo and asks 'What's in a name?'.

One of Stephen's first sallies (9.130–5) in his presentation of Shakespeare links the final body count in *Hamlet* ('Nine lives are taken off for his father's one') to the violence of British imperialism ('khaki Hamlets don't hesitate to shoot') by way of the concentration camps setup during the Boer War. He goes on to set the seventeenth-century scene – 'Canvasclimbers who sailed with Drake chew their sausages among the groundlings' – before positing Shakespeare on the stage (9.164–73), choosing to play the part not of the troubled young Hamlet but rather of the ghost of the old king, addressing his dead son Hamnet (the child of the playwright who died aged 11). It follows, if Shakespeare identified with the ghost of the dead king, that Ann Hathaway is the adulteress queen. Shakespeare's seduction by her and the breakdown of their marriage as a result of her adultery become traumatic influences on his writing (9.454–64) and reconciliation only comes with the birth of a granddaughter (9.421–35).

Stephen broadens the interconnectedness of Shakespeare's life with his plays, referring to other dramas in ways that pointedly debunk bardolatry (9.741–60): *The Merchant of Venice* cashes in on contemporary anti-semitism, the history plays are unashamedly chauvinistic and *The Tempest* – the representation of Caliban sharing the racist stereotype of the stage Irishman ('Patsy Caliban') – colludes with colonialist sentiments. Stephen then returns to *Hamlet*. Ann Hathaway ruins her marriage by sexual liaisons with her brothers-in-laws Edmund and Richard (9.983–92) and the suffering it causes her husband reverberates through his plays (9.997–1015). He dramatises his own life experiences in a way that is psychoanalytically common to us all: 'We walk through ourselves, meeting robbers, ghosts, giants, old men, young men, wives, widows, brothers-in-love, but always meeting ourselves.' (9.1044–6)

Stephen's presentation is listened to politely by his audience of Anglo-Irish intellectuals but his point of view directly opposes their more rarefied and ahistorical understanding of Shakespeare. For A. E. it is a matter of principle – 'Art has to reveal to us ideas, formless spiritual essences' (9.48–49) – and Best agrees with him in considering the artist's biography to be largely irrelevant when appreciating the work. Lyster sees Shakespeare as 'the beautiful ineffectual dreamer' (9.9–10) not the sexually wounded figure that emerges from Stephen's account. Underlying much of what Stephen (and Joyce) is driven to oppose are the cultural politics of the Anglo-Irish, and its embracing of a bardolatry that stressed the purified Englishness of Shakespeare, as well as the elitist and unworldly aesthetics of the Irish Literary Revival.[18] While this helps account for the aggressiveness with which Stephen sets out to debunk idealized notions of the playwright there is also a very positive force behind Stephen's pluralist account that celebrates the richness and lyricism of Shakespeare's language. Joyce's wide range of references to the plays is at its most impressive at the textual level, including those occasions when he mimics and reworks words, phrases and lines from the original, and there is no mistaking the enjoyment he takes in Shakespeare's mastery of language even though he seeks to attack the discourse of British cultural nationalism.

WANDERING ROCKS

Time

3 p.m.

Place

The streets of Dublin

Plot

This chapter is composed of nineteen sections, most of which contain interpolations relating to other events occurring at the same time but in other parts of the city. This breakdown lists the sections and the interpolations:

Section 1 (10.1–205): Father John Conmee, a Jesuit priest, is travelling to a school in Artane to see about a place there for the eldest son of the late Patrick Dignam. Before boarding a tram he meets on the street the wife of Mr David Sheehy MP and then Mrs McGuinness a pawnbroker. Disembarking, he walks along Malahide Road and thinks of older times, the book he could write and of the countess of Belvedere who was imprisoned on an estate by her husband who suspected her of adultery with his brother.

The interpolation (10.56–60) relates to a dancing teacher, Mr Denis J. Maginni, passing Lady Maxwell on a street.

Section 2 (10.207–26): Corny Kelleher, a police tout who works for an undertaker, is standing by his premises when Constable 57C passes by and cryptically refers to an event of the evening before.

Two interpolations (10.213–4 and 10.222–3) mention Father Conmee boarding his tram and a coin being flung (by Molly Bloom) from a window in Eccles Street.

Section 3 (10.228–56): A one-legged sailor in Eccles St has a coin flung to him from a window of No 7 (Bloom's house).

The interpolation (10.236–7) mentions J. J. O'Molloy and Mr Lambert (see section 8).

Section 4 (10.258–97): Katey and Boody, two sisters of Stephen, return home from a failed attempt to pawn some books with Mrs McGuinness. Maggy, their older sister, tells them that another sister, Dilly, has gone to meet their father (see section 11).

Interpolations mention Father Conmee (10.264–5), the ringing of a bell in the auction room where Dilly will meet her father (10.281–2, see section 11) and a flyer about a gospel meeting (10.294–7, perhaps the same one Bloom threw off O'Connell Bridge in 'Lestrygonians') floating down the river Liffey (also mentioned in section 13).

Section 5 (10.299–336): Blazes Boylan is in a shop arranging for the delivery of a basket of fruit.

The interpolation (10.315–6) refers presumably to Bloom, although he is not mentioned by name, looking at books on a hawker's cart (see section 10).

Section 6 (10.338–66): Stephen converses with Almadano Artifoni, an Italian music teacher who urges him not to neglect his fine singing voice.

Section 7 (10.368–96): Miss Dunne, the secretary in Blazes Boylan's office, speaks to her employer on the phone. It is in this section that the reader learns the date is 16 June 1904.

There are two one-sentence interpolations: the first (10.373–4) describes a movement in a machine invented by Tom Rochford (see section 9); the second refers to the sandwich-board men advertising Hely's stationary store (10.377–9).

Section 8 (10.398–463): Ned Lambert (who was with Simon Dedalus in the 'Aeolus' chapter), a seed merchant, is talking to Rev Hugh C. Love, a Church of Ireland clergyman, in a seed store which incorporates the old chapter house of the tenth-century St Mary's

Abbey. They are joined by J. J. O'Molloy (also last seen in the 'Aeolus' chapter).

The first interpolation (10.425) refers to John Howard Parnell (see section 16); the second (10.440–1) to the woman seen by Father Conmee in section 1 (10.201–2).

Section 9 (10.465–583): Tom Rochford (who was in the pub in the 'Lestrygonians' chapter) is showing his invention, a device for indicating to a music hall audience the programme item currently on stage, to Lenehan (the sports journalist from the 'Aeolus' chapter), M'Coy (who met Bloom in the 'Lotus Eaters' chapter) and Nosey Flynn (also in the pub in 'Lestrygonians'). Lenehan says he will mention it to Blazes Boylan, who is a concert promoter, when he meets him in the Ormond Hotel. Lenehan and M'Coy leave, talking about Rochford's heroic rescue of a man from a sewer, and they spot Bloom looking at books from a hawker's cart.

The first interpolation (10.470–5) refers to legal professionals outside a court building; the second (10.515–6) to the viceregal cavalcade (see section 19); the third (10.534–5) to a son of the late Patrick Dignam (see section 18); and the last (10.542–3) to Molly Bloom putting a room-to-let notice back in the window of her house (see section 3).

Section 10 (10.585–641): Bloom is looking for a suitable book for Molly (she asked for one in the 'Calypso' chapter).

There are two interpolations (10.599–600 and 10.625–31), referring to Mr Maginni (see section 1) and a member of the legal profession (see section 9).

Section 11 (10.643–716): Dilly Dedalus, Stephen's sister, meets her father outside Dillon's auction rooms. She asks him for money and he reluctantly gives her some.

An event at the Trinity College Sports day (10.651–3) is the subject of the first interpolation; Tom Kernan (see section 12) of the second (10.673–4) and the viceregal cavalcade (see section 19) the third (10.709–10).

Section 12 (10.718–98): Tom Kernan, a tea merchant, is feeling pleased with himself over an order he secured and his complacency is only disturbed when he realizes he has missed seeing the viceregal cavalcade.

The first interpolation (10.740–1) refers to Simon Dedalus meeting Father Cowley (see section 14); the second (10.752–4) to the flyer already mentioned in section 4); the third (10.778–80) to the odd Denis Breen, whose wife Bloom met in 'Lestrygonians'.

Section 13 (10.800–80): Stephen meets his sister Dilly who has just bought a French primer.

Both of this section's interpolations refer to people already known to the reader: the first (10.818–20) mentions the two women Stephen saw on the beach in the 'Proteus' chapter (3.29–34); Father Conmee and his journey is the subject of the second (10.842–3).

Section 14 (10.882–954): Simon Dedalus meets Father Cowley, a lapsed priest, whose debt to Reuben J. Dodd (the subject of Bloom's attempt to tell a funny story in the funeral carriage) is being pursued by the Jew. They are joined by a mutual acquaintance, Ben Dollard, who assures Cowley that Dodd's writ cannot harm him because his landlord has the first claim on his property.

The second interpolation (10.928–31) mentions Cowley's landlord, the Rev High C. Love; the first one (10.919–20) concerns the eccentric Cashel Boyle O'Connor Fitzmaurice Tisdall Farrell (first mentioned in 'Lestrygonians', 8.295–303).

Section 15 (10: 956–1041): Two of the men who were with Bloom in the funeral carriage, Martin Cunningham and Mr Power, are talking with a friend, John Wyse, about a collection for the family of the deceased Dignam. They meet a Jimmy Henry and the city sub-sheriff Long John Fanning. Their talk is interrupted by the noise of the viceregal cavalcade.

The first interpolation (10.962–3) refers to two barmaids who are not introduced until the next chapter (11.65–66) the second one (10.970–1) refers to the head printer Nannetti (from the 'Aeolus' chapter); and the third one (10.984–5) mentions Blazes Boylan.

Section 16 (10.1043–99): Mulligan and Haines, talking of Stephen, are having tea together.

The interpolations refer to the one-legged sailor (10.1063–4) and the flyer in the river (10.1096–9).

Section 17 (10.1101–20): The music teacher Artifoni, the Cashel Boyle character and the blind young man are walking in the same direction until Cashel Boyle turns around and brushes against the blind man.

Section 18 (1122–74): Young Patrick Dignam is walking home with some pork-steaks.

Section 19 (1176–1282): The viceroy, representative of British rule in Ireland, sets out on a cavalcade through Dublin to inaugurate a bazaar.

Discussion

This chapter records what Bloom and Stephen are doing in the middle of the afternoon but their existences are accorded no more meaning than the accounts presented of the many other characters going about their quotidian business at around the same time. This sense of multiple lives crisscrossing in time and space is accentuated by the interpolations that continually remind the reader that the various narratives are only cross-sections in the life of the city and that the whole is defined by its parts. The usual experience for the reader of a novel when presented with a series of apparently unrelated characters and incidents, whether in a late Dickens work or a complex modern thriller, is to keep them on hold in the knowledge that gradually the jigsaw pieces will connect and the whole picture will be revealed. Usually too, the seemingly unrelated parts are unfolded in the early chapters of the book; here, instead, we have all the parts coming in one chapter in the very middle of the book. And although some connections will be made and can be guessed at – Boylan is buying a present for the woman whose outstretched arm throws a coin to the one-legged sailor – most of the mini-episodes remain unplotted. Miss Dunne plays no further part in the novel; we learn nothing more about Father Conmee or Maginni or Artifoni; and the fate of Dignam's son or Stephen's poor sisters is never made known. Minor characters who have appeared or been mentioned earlier – Corny Kelleher, J. J. O'Molloy, Ned Lambert, Simon Dedalus, Cunningham, Power, M'Coy and Lenehan – are either never heard of again or remain minor figures. The form of the novel traditionally allows for a high value to be placed on dialogue, with particular conversations invested with consequences for one or more character, but the talk in 'Wandering Rocks' remains inconsequential.

Is there, then, no nucleus or whole, so that the chapter functions as microcosm of the decentred metropolitan experience? Individuals move across an urban landscape, pursuing whatever they pursue, sometimes meeting but never in significant ways. The classic account of this way of situating 'Wandering Rocks' within a modernist aesthetics is to be found in an essay by Clive Hart.[19] And there are snatches of everyday conversation or passages like the one about the young Patrick Dignam (10.1165–74) that do not need to be justified in plot terms; they are moments that carry conviction because they capture something about the way life is lived. At the same time, though, a sense emerges of the different sections contributing to an overall picture of the city's life and the fact that the chapter's beginning and end is framed by the twin presences of Church and State – the two masters that Stephen saw himself as subject to in 'Telemachus' – gives a clue to what is going on. The complacent Father Conmee makes his way across the city as does the viceroy and his entourage but Joyce quietly questions their authority. Sensuality resists the priest's spirituality by way of the young woman's 'wild nodding daisies' and the 'slow care' with which she detaches a twig from her skirt as she emerges from a hedge with her partner, (10.199–202). Reactions to the viceroy are also muted and the occasionally loyal responses are wickedly counterpointed by other gestures: Simon Dedalus, emerging from a toilet with the buttons of his trousers possibly undone (10.1200–1), may inadvertently have made a display as rude as the River Poddle's 'tongue of liquid sewage' hung out 'in fealty' (10.1197); Parnell's brother pointedly pays more attention to a game of chess (10.1226); blank stares are not uncommon (10.1230, 1260, 1261).

Unlike many of the book's details the viceregal cavalcade was not based on a real event of the 16 June 1904 and Joyce introduced it – Budgen saw him working 'with a map of Dublin before him on which were traced in red ink the paths of the Earl of Dudley and Father Conmee'[20] – as a means of articulating and amplifying the capital's landscape as a colonial city. 'Wandering Rocks' is constructed around the distribution of power, the determinate formations of Dublin's citizens as colonial subjects and the ways these positions are experienced at a personal level. Bloom and Stephen are both outsiders, they do not feature in the chapter's final section, though Stephen registers his colonial status when he identifies a group of English tourists (in 1904 they can hardly be non-British) as 'Palefaces' (10.341).[21] Other characters are caught up in shifting relationships of power that require constant negotiation, whether it be the obsequious Tom Kernan, the humble shop assistant dealing with Boylan, Ned Lambert ingratiating himself with the Protestant clergyman or the powerless Lenehan pathetically attempting to bolster his self-image with his tale about Molly Bloom (10.566–74). They are like voyagers facing the wandering rocks – a challenge that Ulysses was able to avoid by taking an alternative route by way of Scylla and Charybdis. It requires a detailed analysis by way of the historical allusions to show how Joyce adroitly weaves patterns of servility and resistance to the colonial order in this chapter but even on a first reading it is clear that 'Wandering Rocks' is taking the reader well beyond the level of psychological verisimilitude in its dissection of Irish society.[22] Although the change is not as sudden and unannounced as some critics make it to be, *Ulysses* does begin to develop in a direction that is more pronounced from around 'Wandering Rocks' onwards and the foregrounding of style, the usual way of describing the difference, becomes very apparent in the next chapter.

SIRENS

Time

4 p.m.

Place

Bar and dining room of the quayside Ormond Hotel.

Plot

The barmaids, bronze-haired Miss Douce and the golden-haired Miss Kennedy, are watching the viceregal cavalcade pass by before sitting down behind the bar for a cup of tea. After Simon Dedalus enters, Lenehan turns up to keep an appointment with Boylan. Bloom, walking along the quayside on the other side of the river, stops to buy stationary and spots Boylan in a carriage in the distance. He follows him to the Ormond Hotel and enters the dining room with Richie Goulding whom he met outside. Boylan leaves the bar with Lenehan as Ben Dollard and Father Cowley enter. As Bloom eats a meal at a table with Goulding he can hear the men singing in the bar. He writes a reply to Marta Clifford. George Lidwell, a solicitor, and Tom Kernan join the company in the bar and Bloom is preparing to leave when Simon Dedalus begins singing 'The Croppy Boy' (about a young rebel in the 1798 rebellion captured by a soldier disguised as a priest listening to his confession). Boylan is arriving at Bloom's house and the blind piano tuner is tapping his way back to the Ormond Hotel where he left his tuning fork. Bloom, having left the bar, breaks wind while reading in a shop window the last words of Robert Emmet (another patriot executed by the British).

Discussion

The Homeric correspondence helps explain why the first 63 lines of this chapter could be skipped on a first reading. Odysseus is forewarned that the song of the two Sirens would lure his ship onto rocks and has his crew stop their ears with wax and himself tied to the mast of his vessel. Following their strict orders not to release him, the crew ignore his desperate pleadings and they sail safely past the singing Sirens. Joyce makes music the subject of 'Sirens' in a rich variety of ways and he begins with a textual overture consisting of phrases taken out of the contexts in which they will occur in the chapter's story. These 63 lines will make little sense at first and could be returned to after having grasped and followed the course of the chapter.

Following the story, like listening to a fugue (the comparison that Joyce offered for the chapter's structure), involves holding different themes together as the text moves between events in the hotel's bar-room and dining room, Boylan's journey to Eccles St and the 'tap' motif of the blind piano tuner. The coda to all of this takes the form of an orchestrated, onomatopoeic act of flatulence, with the word '*Done*' indicating more than just an expulsion of air. It signals the chapter's end, just as 'Begin!' in line 63 announces its start, and as well as being the final word of Robert Emmet's speech from the dock ('When my country takes her place among the nations of the earth, then, and not till then, let my epitaph be written. I have done.') it can be seen as registering the act of infidelity taking place in Eccles St. Bloom's awareness of this impending act has been preoccupying him throughout the chapter and after leaving the hotel he knows that the adulterous deed is done.

Music is obviously at the heart of this most acoustic chapter but different critical approaches choose to dwell on those aspects that support their particular way of reading literary texts. Indeed, different interpretations of this chapter offer a potted history of *Ulysses* criticism over the past few decades. Liberal humanism, using the term without disparagement, focuses on Bloom's marital relationship and finds it modulated through the music he listens to in the bar. Hence the song from the opera *Martha* (11.658–751), about a love believed to have been lost and the deep longing this provokes for Martha's return, becomes inseparable from Bloom's memories of happy times with Molly and his troubled awareness of what is about to happen when Boylan arrives at his house. His anxiety recurs during the singing of 'The Croppy Boy' when the solitary plight of the young rebel, whose father and brothers have died in the fighting, causes Bloom to reflect on the fact that he and Molly no longer have sex: 'I too. Last of my race. Milly young student. Well, my fault perhaps. No son, Rudy. Too late now. Or if not? If not? If still?' (11.1066–7). Bloom's Ulysses-like wisdom, his ability to resist the Sirens' call, is seen in his capacity to not fall prey to self-pity, not to stop loving Molly nor self-indulgently surrender to music's balm. He leaves the hotel before the song is over, glad to avoid the backslapping aftermath (11.1139–45): 'Freer in air. Music. Gets on your nerves' (11.1182). His musical fart while reading the last words of the condemned patriot is interpreted as an act of resistance to the emotional appeal of militant patriotism.

A language-centred approach of a purist kind puts character analysis to one side and stresses what is seen as the chapter's self-conscious experimenting with writing, a process that disrupts narrative coherence in the interests of tuning language so that it emulates the musical. The text is seen to exhibit an aural logic and a textual exuberance that expresses itself in musical puns and verbal games (like the tinkering with 'greatest alacrity' in lines 213–17).[23] The lure of the Sirens translates into a seduction theme that shapes the language; and in the passage describing Lydia Douce's response to the singing of 'The Croppy Boy' in a way that remarkably blends the erotic and the comic, the musical and the voyeuristic:

> On the smooth jutting beerpull laid Lydia hand, lightly, plumply, leave it to my hands. All lost in pity for croppy. Fro, to: to, fro: over the polished knob (she knows his eyes, my eyes, her eyes) her thumb and finger passed in pity: passed, reposed and, gently touching, then slid so smoothly, slowly down, a cool firm white enamel baton protruding through their sliding ring. (11.1110–17)

The theory of Lacanian psychoanalysis joins forces with deconstruction to offer a different take on the way language operates on 'Sirens'.[24] MacCabe, for example, sees an opposition in the chapter between the materiality of writing and the voice's imaginary unity of a self. The chapter's play with the practice of writing exposes the terms of difference, at the level of both letters and words, that constitute meaning – examples being Aaron Figatner's name triggering 'Figather? Gathering figs I think' (11. 149–50) or Father Cowley thinking 'He saved the situa. Tight trou. Brilliant ide' (11.483–4) – and thereby undermines the sense of untainted presence offered by a pure voice like that of the Sirens. Bloom's writing of a letter while others are lured by the singing voice focuses attention on the activity of reading, and the chapter's concern to show the signifier as no longer effaced has been seen to carry a political import. The imaginary unity offered by the voice is allied to the appeal of nationalism in 'The Croppy Boy'; sentimental patriotism being another discourse that tries to fix meanings and subjectivities by a fictional and paralyzing communion with the past, the illusion of 'endlessnessnessness' (11.750). Like so many theory-led readings of *Ulysses*, a post-structuralist interpretation risks being too partial for its own good and an insistence on a writing/voice opposition as the chapter's key necessarily ignores other readings that point to textual and political complexities not easily contained by this insistence.[25]

CYCLOPS

Time

5 p.m.

Place

Barney Kiernan's pub

Plot

The unnamed narrator, a debt collector, meets the journalist Joe Hynes and they enter Barney Kiernan's pub where the narrator wants to speak to a man known as the citizen. Bob Doran, awaking from a drunken sleep, is also in the pub and Alf Bergen arrives to join the company and show some letters of application from hangmen that he possesses. Bloom, who has arranged to meet with Martin Cunningham in the pub prior to visiting the Dignam family, waits outside until the citizen prevails upon him to come inside. After the entrance of J. J. O'Molloy and Ned Lambert the citizen's hostility towards Bloom becomes more apparent as he makes some antisemitic remarks. Two more men, Lenehan and John Wyse Nolan, enter the pub and Bloom, flustered by the tone that the conversation is taking, leaves to look for Cunningham. A horse called Throwaway (inadvertently tipped by Bloom in 'Lotus Eaters') has won that day's Gold Cup and Lenehan thinks Bloom has left to collect his winnings from a bookmaker. Cunningham arrives with two friends and when Bloom returns the four of them set about leaving together. The citizen, now aggressively anti-semitic and angered by Bloom's ripostes, hurls a biscuit tin at him and his dog gives chase.

Discussion

In the *Odyssey* Odysseus and his men find themselves in a cave at the mercy of a one-eyed monster from the race of the Cyclops. Odysseus plies him with wine and when he falls asleep he is blinded with a burning stake, allowing Odysseus and his men to escape back to their ship. The vengeful giant hurls a rock at them into the sea and it just misses Odysseus's vessel. For a long time the Homeric correspondence has been understood didactically : Bloom is the hero who stands up for his values against a stronger force and the xenophobic citizen is the cannibalistic giant outwitted by someone more civilized than himself. The citizen represents belligerent nationalism and Bloom's pacifist but firm resistance becomes an ethical act of humanist, liberal defiance.

The troubling limitation with this kind of literary algebra is that like the plot summary above it sidelines what is the most obvious feature of the chapter's text, the impossible-to-ignore interruptions to the narrative that take off and follow their own stylistic flight paths. They are as clearly different in nature from the interpolations in 'Wandering Rocks' as they are from the other narrative voice in this chapter, the unknown Dubliner in the bar who bears witness to the conversations and events taking place around him. As early as 1956 Hugh Kenner noted the background presence in the interpolations of key Irish Literary Revival texts but a fuller historically informed analysis, having passed through a post-structuralist detour, had to wait nearly half a century.[26] Far from being a set of freewheeling discourses, playing with different ways of signifying the world and denying the closure that a meta-narrative could offer, it seems clear that various discourses of the Anglo-Irish intelligentsia, especially historiographical ones, are the satiric target of many of the interruptions. The revivalist accounts of Irish history, with their ancient bards and lists and double-epitheted heroes, evoke a mythical era in the country's history and Joyce mercilessly mocks them for their nostalgia and the falsity of their claim to a purity of the racial spirit. Instead of noble Cuchulain and his trusty hound we are given the citizen and his revolting but verse-reciting dog Garryowen and throughout the chapter the fabricated romanticism of the revivalist project is comically exposed by ridiculing its discourses. There is a family resemblance between the poetic diction of idealized and declamatory translations of ancient sagas, the falsifying language of an affected journalese and the revivalist vogue for the theosophical, and countering the interpolations head-on is the demotic culture of Dublin in all its vibrant, biting and often dire orality. The Dublin argot is not parodied; on the contrary, chiefly but not always through the voice of the anonymous narrator, its verve positions it outside the splenetic exaggerations of the citizen's language. This narrator considers the citizen a 'bloody clown' (12.1794) and to Joe Hynes is given a marvellously concise and historically precise – the very qualities deficient in revivalist historiography – condemnation of the German-based monarchy ruling Ireland: 'And as for those Proo-shians and the Hanovarians, says Joe, haven't we had enough of those sausageeating bastards on the throne from George the elector down to the German lad and the flatulent old bitch that's dead?' (12.1390–2).

Bloom himself, when he shows a lamentable lack of precision in opposing the citizen with talk of love, is subjected to ridicule for his failure to find a *mot juste*:

> Love loves to love love. Nurse loves the new chemist. Constable 14 A loves Mary Kelly. Gerty MacDowell loves the boy that has the bicycle. M.B. loves a fair gentleman. Li Chi Han lovey up kissy Cha Pu Chow. Jumbo, the elephant, loves Alice, the elephant .... You love a certain person. And this person loves that other person because everybody loves somebody but God loves everybody. (12.1493–501)

The citizen is not as ignorant as he is often portrayed by critics – some of his historical judgements were shared by Joyce – but his means of expression, his polarizing discourse, is as limited and ineffectual as the pseudo-histories of the Revival. His anti-semitism chimes with the ethnic nationalism that he espouses so virulently and when he is funny, as in his murderous response to Bloom telling him Christ was a Jew --'By Jesus, I'll crucify him so I will' (12.1812), the humour escapes him.

NAUSICAA

Time

8 p.m.

Place

Sandymount Strand

Plot

Three girls, Cissy Caffrey, Edy Boardman and Gerty MacDowell, are on the beach with Cissy's young twin brothers and Edy's baby brother. Bloom, who has been visiting the Dignam house nearby, is also on the beach and he and Gerty become aware of one another. When the other two girls leave with the children to see the fireworks coming from the Mirus bazaar Gerty and Bloom are left alone. There is a short distance between them and as Gerty leans back to view a firework, exposing her legs and underwear, Bloom masturbates. He remains on the beach after Gerty's departure.

Discussion

The first 770 lines can be called Gerty's discourse and although it is not a first-person account it is her consciousness that is on show. The writing employs the genteel diction of Edwardian pulp fiction for women to create a style that Joyce described as 'namby-pamby, jammy marmalady'[27]. This half of the chapter is taken by many to be a satire of sentimental romance fiction and while it can certainly be enjoyed at this level the result tends to suggest derision on Joyce's part and a view of Gerty as merely the product of a particular discursive formation. She becomes a verbal construct, defined by the style that is seen to constitute her subjectivity, and of severely limited interest as a character in her own right.[28] As with any part of *Ulysses*, however, there is always more going on than at first appears and there are always questions emerging from the text. Gerty is almost the same age as Stephen Dedalus and she is on the beach that he walked along in 'Proteus'. She shares some of his characteristics – an interest in learning, a desire to be free, a sensual yearning – and partly parodies if not shares his aspirations.[29] The writing style does enact her identification with the imported ideal of English feminine beauty found in the fiction and advertisements from women's magazines but there are intrusions in the vernacular mode that point to a more individualized consciousness, one that is not defined by the models that fill her fantasy space:

> Her hands were of finely veiled alabaster with tapering fingers and as white as lemon juice and queen of ointments could make them though it was not true that she used to wear kid gloves in bed or take a milk footbath either. Bertha Supple told that once to Edy Boardman, a deliberate lie, when she was black out at daggers drawn with Gerty . . . . There was an innate refinement, a languid queenly *hauteur* about Gerty which was unmistakably evidenced in her delicate hands and higharched instep. (13.89–98)

Many of the details in Gerty's discourse can be traced back to the language of Victorian- and Edwardian-era advertisements for women – 'queen of ointments' was a slogan for Beetham's skin cream – and beauty products were regularly promoted in the two women's magazines that are mentioned in 'Nausicaa', *The Princess's Novelettes* and *Lady's Pictorial*. The pursuit of pure white skin, an ideal which carried a racial overtone in these magazines, brings Bertha Supple's mischief-making to Gerty's mind and her annoyance is expressed in her colloquial use of black as an intensifier and the idiom of daggers being drawn. Gerty's spontaneity briefly surfaces here and the spat she remembers is unselfconsciously at odds with the 'innate refinement' that she might like to think she possesses. There is an alertness to Gerty, subtly conveyed perhaps in the slang meaning of '*hauteur*'[30], that serves to remind us of an impoverished girl's existence and her desire for something other.

The second half of 'Nausicaa' returns to Bloom's interior monologue for the last time in any length. It helps in getting to the heart of what makes Bloom such an engaging character if one bears in mind Joyce's critical response to a friend's notion of art:

> in realism you are down to facts on which the world is based: that sudden reality which smashes romanticism into a pulp. What makes most people's lives unhappy is some disappointed romanticism, some unrealizable or misconceived ideal . . . Nature is quite

unromantic. It is we who put romance into her, which is a false attitude, an egotism, absurd like all egotisms.[31]

Bloom is not an egotist and there is a matter-of-factness about his reflections on what has taken place with Gerty and what has occurred with Boylan and Molly – 'O, he did. Into her. She did. Done.' (13.849) – just around the time his watch stopped working. He recalls the fact that shark liver oil is used to clean watches and then rearranges his semen-wetted shirt. He is not callous or indifferent, deciding to visit Mrs Dignam in hospital and, as always, thinking happily of Molly, but accepts the contingencies and coincidences of life. The sense of tranquillity expressed in the deftly poised ending to this chapter parallels its opening paragraph but the gap separating them is the distance between romanticism and realism.

OXEN OF THE SUN

Time

10 p.m.

Place

National Maternity Hospital, 29–31 Holles St

Plot

Bloom arrives at the hospital and after asking about a Dr O'Hare that he used to know, now deceased (14.94–106), enquires about Mrs Purefoy and learns that she is still in labour (14.111–22). Bloom meets a Dr Dixon, who once treated him for a bee sting, and is invited to join some company for a drink (14.123–140). Lenehan is there (last seen in 'Cyclops') with a group of medical students – Vincent Lynch, Madden, Francis 'Punch' Costello and Crotthers – and Stephen Dedalus. After discussing whether a pregnant woman's life should be saved at the cost of aborting her child (14.202–59) the conversation becomes more bawdy until a loud crack of thunder frightens Stephen and Bloom attempts to calm him (14.408–28).

After a lengthy chat arising from mention of foot-and-mouth disease (14.529–650), Mulligan arrives with Alec Bannon and more lewd chat ensures. Mulligan gives a lurid account of Haines turning up at the literary soirée that was mentioned in 'Scylla and Charybdis' (14.1010–37). Discomforted, Bloom reflects on his own youth and his son who died (14.1038–77) before imagining a strange scene of animals moving across an arid landscape (14.1078–109) and a vision of feminine radiance in the sky that morphs into a ruby-coloured triangle. This is the red triangle on a bottle of Bass beer and Bloom, awakening to his situation, pours out a glass for Lenehan (14.1174–97) and converses with the company about gender and infant mortality (14.1223–309). Stephen's bitterness concerns Bloom and he remembers the first time he saw him as a child at a garden party (14.1356–78). Everyone takes off to Burke's pub (14.1391) where Stephen buys two rounds of drinks. At some stage Mulligan slips away to meet Haines at the railway station (14.1027) for the journey back to the tower, leaving Stephen in the lurch (14.1536–40). Stephen and Lynch set off for a train to the red-light district and Bloom goes with them (14.1572–5).

Discussion

This chapter, when first reading it, is an especially difficult chapter to get to grips with because the narrative is so embedded in a series of English prose styles that it becomes impossible to separate style from content. The episode starts with three, thrice-repeated invocations: a Latin–Irish call to 'let us go to the right at Holles St' (14.1), a fertility call to the sun (a chief doctor at Holles St hospital was Alexander Horne) and a midwife's cry at birth (14.5–6). The following three paragraphs use Latin syntax and vocabulary, explaining the importance of childbirth provision, specifically with the Celts, followed by a passage emulating Anglo-Saxon prose and then Middle English and so on. By the end of the chapter the prose is employing a conflation of Pidgin English, Cockney, slang and doggerel; ending in a gospel style sparked by the evangelical poster that was passed by Stephen, Lynch and Bloom. The editions of *Ulysses* published by Penguin and Oxford World Classics indicate in their notes where the various changes of prose style occur; indicating, for example, how the style of Thomas Mallory informs lines 167–276, John Bunyan's

Pilgrim's Progress is at work in 429–73, various eighteenth-century essayists like Edmund Burke in 845–79, De Quincey at 1078–1109, Dickens at 1310–43, John Ruskin at 1379–90 and so on.

The reader, caught between following the changes of style and trying to discern the plot narrative, is equally bedevilled when it comes to feeling sure about the nature of any significance that might arise from the chapter's stylistic voyage through English prose. For a long time, Joyce's remark in a letter to Budgen about the chapter's Homeric correspondence has been taken at face-value in this respect. Homer's tale of how Odysseus' men slaughter sacred cattle on an island only to be punished by having their ship destroyed and drowning provides the idea, wrote Joyce, of contraception being a crime against fecundity and how 'Bloom is the spermatozoon, the hospital the womb, the nurse the ovum, Stephen the embryo. How's that for high?'[32] Joyce's final flourish here suggests a lack of seriousness but it has not prevented Ellmann, for example, reading the chapter's opening style as fascistic in its Latinate forms but brought down to earth with Bloom's entrance and then the tracing of orderly development in prose over the centuries. The chapter's concluding style – the mélange of slang and doggerel that starts at line 1440 – is viewed as 'placental outpouring . . . . not yet subject to artistic form' and, like the excessive order of the opening style, to be contrasted with the organic development of English that unfolds between these two extremes.[33]

Ellmann's reading of the chapter's final stylistic foray, however unconvincing, does have the virtue of getting around the basic problem presented by any simple analogy between the growth of the foetus and the historical development of the English language. Such a correspondence suggests a progressive movement of gestation: the act of birth completing a natural, nine-month course and the growth of English prose maturing though time to reach its apogee of expression. Such a teleology rather collapses with the last stage of the chapter's stylistic adventure given that the pastiche of American revivalism can hardly sustain the symbolic import that would attach to a movement mirroring the creative climax of birth:

Alexander J Christ Dowie, that's my name, that's yanked to glory most half this planet from Frisco beach to Vladivostok. The Deity aint no nickel dime bumshow. I put it to you that He's on the square and a corking fine business proposition. He's the grandest thing yet and don't you forget it. (14.1584–8)

For some critics, it is the ultimate absence of a progressive movement in the styles of 'Oxen of the Sun' that points towards the chapter's significance. Joyce charts a chronological, historically determined course to the gestation of English male prose (no women writers are included) but one that is devoid of a positive meaning or a sense of a literary tradition maturing over time. Joyce is seen to be negating the English literary tradition by rifling anthologies – he worked chiefly from George Sainsbury's *A History of English Prose Rhythm* (1912) and William Peacock's *English Prose from Mandeville to Ruskin* (1903)[34] – and producing parodies that undermine notions of a progressive tradition. The parodies are exercised in a spirit of comedy and so we have Stephen, the embryo fertilized by Bloom according to Joyce's letter, coming into life towards the chapter's end with the vagitus – the cry of the new-born – to visit the nearest pub: 'Burke's!' (14.1391).

While parody can be read as a form of flattery and the 'Oxen of the Sun' chapter seen as a comic form of respect for the English writers whose styles are invoked, this is not what comes across in Joyce's writing. He plays with the different styles to suit his own mischievous sense of humour and so, for example, in the passage after the style of Oliver Goldsmith (14.799–844) there are eighteenth-century locutions like 'Gad's bud' (14.808) for God's body and 'Demme' (14.810) for damn but also 'if she ain't in the family way' (14.817) and the Cockney grammar of 840–4. Such hybridity is characteristic of an author who, far from being in thrall to the source material he worked from in Sainsbury's and Peacock's anthologies, confidently and comically mines it for his own anarchic and mimetic purpose.[35] T. S. Eliot may have put it too dogmatically when he said to Virginia Woolf that *Ulysses* had 'destroyed the whole of the 19th century . . . . It showed up the futility of all English styles', sidestepping the acknowledgement that Joyce is paying to the various prose styles and ignoring the laughter that animates his contradictory engagement with and alienation from the language of imperial Britain. At the same time, though, there is a sense in the 'Oxen of the Sun' that Joyce is deliberately breaching boundaries and highlighting cultural differences in a way that is subversive. The final stylistic movement glides from a pastiche of Thomas Carlyle (1775–1881) to a Babel of what Joyce described as 'a frightful jumble of pidgin English, nigger English, Cockney, Irish, Bowery slang and broken doggerel'[36], making the final voice heard not that of an eminent Victorian essayist but one who is diasporic and marginalized.

CIRCE

Time

12 midnight

Place

The brothel area of Dublin and Bella Cohen's brothel in Tyrone Street

Plot

Cissy Caffrey and Edy Boardman are apparently in the brothel quarter and two British soldiers named Carr and Compton are making their way towards it, as are Stephen and Lynch. Bloom has lost sight of Stephen (15.635–9) and in the rush of pursuit is almost knocked over by a council cleaning vehicle (15.174–7). A series of fantasies follow, beginning with the appearance of a nameless figure (15.212), Bloom's father and mother, followed by Molly, some prostitutes, Gerty MacDowell and then Mrs Breen.

Bloom feeds a dog before another fantasy scene unfolds (15.675–1267) with Bloom on trial for various offences, chiefly sexual misdemeanours. The courtroom fades away and Bloom reaches Bella Cohen's brothel where, after conversing with the prostitute Zoe (15.1283–352), he is extravagantly honoured by fellow Dubliners (15.1364–618) and damned by others (15.1712–62). Bloom gives birth to eight children (15.1821) before he is set on fire and dies a martyr.

Zoe brings Bloom into the music room of the brothel where Stephen is expostulating with Lynch (15.2087–2124). Various personages manifest themselves, including Bloom's grandfather (15.2304) and Stephen's father (15.2654). The madam of the brothel, Bella Cohen, enters and her speaking fan subdues Bloom before Bella changes into the masculine Bello and humiliates Bloom, now a maidservant, with demeaning tasks (15.2835–3218). The nymph whose image hangs over his bed in Eccles St materializes until the breaking of a button on Bloom's trousers (15.3439) signals a restoration of his more normal self. He gets back his potato talisman, given earlier to Zoe, and helps Stephen settle the bill before a reading of palms leads into a fantasy featuring Bloom the flunkey enjoying a sexual escapade between Molly and Boylan (15.3756–816).

There follows (15.3820–4004) various exchanges between Stephen, Lynch, Bloom and the prostitutes, with Simon Dedalus appearing as a bird and also featuring a foxhunt with a rider less dark horse and the school principal Garret Deasy. With the playing of 'My Girl's a Yorkshire Girl' a dance gets underway (15.4005–154), until Stephen's mother appears in a ghastly guise. An anguished Stephen argues with the apparition of his mother before breaking a chandelier with his stick and it is left to Bloom to settle Bella's claim for compensation.

Bloom leaves the brothel to follow Stephen and becomes involved in Stephen's encounter with two British soldiers. Edward VII is among the crowd of onlookers (15.4459) and, after Stephen is knocked down by one of the soldiers, two constables arrive. Bloom is left with a semi-unconscious Stephen and a vision of his dead son Rudy, now aged eleven, smiling but not seeing his father.

Discussion

Differing ways of reading 'Circe' reflect the divide between Leavisite humanist criticism, with its basis in the individual's subjectivity, and historically minded studies rooted in the colonial relationship between Ireland and England in the 1880–1920 period. Until fairly recently, a Freudian approach has informed the reception of 'Circe', viewing the hallucinatory nature of the chapter's events as a dream-like rendition of interiority: repressed fears and desires coming to the surface for shape- and role-changing enactments on the stage of the psyche. Paralleling the night-time dreamer recycling troubling aspects of the past, 'Circe' returns to the text of *Ulysses* and reconfigures moments that remain unresolved. In this way the unknown man first seen at the funeral in 'Hades', mistakenly named Macintosh (6.891–4), reappears to point an accusing finger at Bloom (15.1560–4)[37]; his very anonymity is a source of discomfort for Bloom and, as such, a symptom of his uncertain sense of self. Other enactments of

Bloom's anxieties, as with the appearance of his dead father and his own transformation from male to female, are more pronounced. An earlier reversal turned Bloom the condemned prisoner, accused of various sexual improprieties, into an acclaimed citizen. Stephen's unconscious is also laid bare, reaching an anguished climax with the appearance of his mother and her warning about eternal damnation.

A psychoanalytic reading of 'Circe' traces a positive trajectory with Bloom emerging from his self-abnegation to defend Stephen against the wily whore mistress and then rescue him after the encounter with the British soldiers. Surrogate father meets surrogate son when Bloom bends over the recumbent young man and, for the first time, addresses him as Stephen. This, it would seem, is a climax in the novel, the meeting of Odysseus with Telemachus, its tremendous psychological import confirmed by the apparition of Rudy. Under-cutting this, though, is the extravagant and sentimental theatricality of Rudy's appearance, with his 'ivory cane with a violet bowknot' and the lamb peeping out of his waistcoat pocket, and the bathos of Stephen's quotation from Yeats's 'Who goes with Fergus?' (sung by him to his dying mother) being misunderstood by Bloom as a reference to some girl, a Miss Ferguson. Hugh Kenner, alert to the distractions from interiority in the chapter's finale, observes of Rudy's apparition: 'What could be more "objective" than a boy whom we can see, in specified costume, reading a Hebrew book? Yet no one sees him at all except ourselves, who are not there but seated in front of a book of English words.'[38]

A concern with the English words of 'Circe' underpins a different appreciation of the chapter in Andrew Gibson's *Joyce's Revenge*. His closely textual analysis draws attention to how the British presence in Ireland resides in Dublin's Anglicized unconscious, the return of the repressed heard in the English voices that permeate the hallucinatory scenes. It is noticeable, for example, how Bloom speaks in a conven-tionally genteel tone of English when Mrs Breen questions his presence in the brothel quarter: 'How do you do? It's ages since I. You're looking splendid. Absolutely it. Seasonable weather we are having this time of year.' (15.399–401). Verbal English proprieties are used as a register of respectability and, for Gibson, 'The truly disruptive Other in "Circe" is not the Freudian id. It is the alien idiom.'[39] The saturnalian excess of 'Circe' is seen as a carnival in Bakhtin's sense of the term, an exuberant travesty of cultural norms, and one that in this context ridicules the effects of an imposed Anglicized culture upon the Irish. The masked face of Matthew Arnold returns (15.2514; first seen in 'Telemachus' (1.172–5), with Philip Drunk and Philip Sober, a non-Freudian transformation of a notable literary figure into a member of Britain's lumpen intelligentsia. In a similarly mocking manner, 'My Girl's a Yorkshire Girl', the song 'blared and drumthumped' during the viceregal procession (10.1249–57), accompanies Stephen's wild hoofing.

It is difficult not to think of 'Circe' in a psychoanalytic way and yet the episode goes well beyond the orthodoxies of a psychological novel. The final scene which brings the chapter to an end is so kitschy that its psychological significance is greatly reduced and, like so much else associated with the various fantasies, has little or no reverberations for the plot or the characters. There is also the curious parody of the Catholic litany which follows the setting afire of Bloom by a member of the Dublin Fire Brigade:

> Kidney of Bloom, pray for us
> Flower of the Bath, pray for us
> Mentor of Menton, pray for us
> Canvasser for the Freeman, pray for us (15.1941–4)

The litany continues for another eight lines, listing various guises of Bloom (mentor, canvasser, Mason and so on) or items associated with him (kidney, soap, potato), in a sequence that follows the chronological order of the episodes from 'Calypso' ('Kidney of Bloom') to 'Circe' ('Potato Preservative against Plague and Pestilence'). It is a summary of Bloom's day but seems to go beyond being a projection of his mind, a dramatization of his interior monologue. It is as if the book *Ulysses* is reflecting and looking back at itself and its presentation of Bloom.

Aspects of the chapter's style have a cinematic quality that has been traced back to Joyce's visits to cinemas in Trieste and his interest in film (see page 4). Early trick films played with animated objects and forms of transformations, just as 'Circe' plays with Bloom's singing bar of soap or madam Bella's talking fan, and it has also been suggested that the linguistic deformations found in *Ulysses* are a version of the visual distortions that characterized the first animated cartoons shown on cinema screens.[40]

EUMAEUS

Time

12.40–1 a.m.

Place

A cabman's shelter at Butt Bridge near the Custom House

Plot

Stephen, exhausted and still not sober, accompanies Bloom to a cabman's shelter where they can rest and have a non-alcoholic drink. They set off to walk, having failed to find a carriage for hire, passing the post of a council watchman named Gumley who knows Stephen's father. Corley, an acquaintance of Stephen, is also there and he borrows money from Stephen. At the cabman's shelter, where a group of Italians are arguing about money, Bloom buys a coffee and bun for his companion and they settle into the shelter's company. A seaman talks of his travels, a prostitute looks in the door, Stephen and Bloom engage in a meandering conversation and the keeper of the shelter blames Britain for Irish problems. Conversation turns to Parnell, Bloom shows Stephen a photograph of Molly and worries about his welfare. Feeling some kinship between them and thinking of ways they could work together, Bloom suggests that Stephen return with him to Eccles St. They set off, with Stephen leaning on the older man's arm, talking about music and others matters as they repeat in reverse the morning walk to the baths.

Discussion

It is not obvious to a first-time reader what to make of this chapter and the nature of the Homeric correspondence is not what it seems to be. In the *Odyssey*, Odysseus finally returns to his island home but in disguise because of the threat posed by the suitors and goes first to the hut of his loyal swineherd Eumaeus. Odysseus reveals his true self to his son and together they plan how to deal with the suitors. The keeper of the cabman's shelter, known as Skin-the-Goat, would seem to be Eumaeus and the long-awaited coming together of Bloom with Stephen, paralleling the meeting of Odysseus and Telemachus, would seem to point the way towards a resolution of some order. Bloom, a father figure without a son, rescues a young man who has a father but lacks a father figure. In the course of the day's odyssey, their paths have crossed more than once and now, finally together, surely they will find some common cause that will cement their new relationship. It is not to be and, given the narrative voice and the style of the chapter's writing, their time together is rendered anti-climatic and at odds with what would be a high point of any classic realist text.

The narrator in 'Eumaeus', an anonymous male Dubliner, delivers his account in a curious, ambulatory fashion, as if not really sure about the accuracy of much of what he reports. And there is much in this episode to be uncertain about, as in Bloom's eulogy of Italian when the language is actually being used vulgarly, or the Simon Dedalus that the sailor claims to know of or the identity of Skin-the-Goat – one James Fitzharris drove a decoy cab away from Phoenix Park, after the 1881 murders of two senior figures in the British administration, but is Skin-the-Goat the same person? Bloom's own identity is questioned in the newspaper report of Dignam's funeral that lists among those attending one 'L. Boom (16.1260).

The uncertainty principle, which governs much of what we read in this chapter, attaches itself to D. B. Murphy, the sailor who regales the company with his tales of travel and adventure. As the worldly wise mariner who has returned home after years of travelling, separated from his wife for seven years (16.419–21), he suggests an Odysseus-like figure but any such expectation is deflated by doubts about his true background – and what is true of the sailor's discourse applies equally to an overall description of the chapter's language: loquacious yet indecisive, often suspect. Sometimes, like the episode's opening: 'Preparatory to anything else', the words are redundant – in one sense, nothing could be anything but preparatory given the opening of a new chapter – but more usually the language is too verbose:

A few moments later saw our two noctambules safely seated in a discreet corner only to be greeted by stares from the decidedly miscellaneous collection of waifs and strays and other nondescript specimens of the genus *homo* already there engaged in eating and drinking diversified by conversation for whom they seemingly formed an object of marked curiosity. (16.325–30)

The narrative is often delivered in a style that the reader has come to associate with Bloom himself and the consciousness of our hero seems to infect the telling. Indeed, this has been called Bloom's chapter on the grounds that it is written in his relaxed idiom, characterized by his clichés, circumlocutions and magpieish knowledge. At the same time, there are important differences and the solecisms and mixed metaphors that characterize the style cannot be reduced solely to a function of character: Bloom is less wordy, not given to so many qualifications, more insightful and interesting than the tentative, unemotional narrator. Perhaps it is Bloom's chapter in the sense that his self-portrait, the way he would like to see himself and be seen by others, emerges from the sometimes stilted prose. Hugh Kenner points to Bloom's praise of Italian (16.334–347) to show how the surfeit of imported phrases and the overdone elegance are seen as intimately related to the kind of man Bloom would like to be.

The play with identity and deception in Books 13–16 of the *Odyssey* can be seen as central to 'Eumaeus' – taking in the dubious provenance of the sailor whom Joyce called Ulysses Psuedoangelos (Ulysses the false messenger) – and helps account for the air of unreliability and mistrust that shrouds much of what is reported. Bloom's own account of his encounter with the citizen (16.1081–7) is, like the newspaper account of Dignam's funeral (16.1248–61), not all it should be. 'Sounds are impostors . . . like names' (16.362), says Stephen, and the critic Marilyn French has noted how deception pervades the language of this episode, accounting for both the difficulty Stephen and Bloom have in communicating with one another and the odd sentence structures to be found.[41] To take this idea further allows for the possibility that the narrative voice is part of this deception, the reader misled into hearing Bloom in this voice when really another impostor is at work. This leaves unresolved the difficulty of fixing on a secure identity for Bloom himself.[42] After all, 'Circe' has shown just how protean is the nature of Bloom's identity and 'it was quite within the bounds of possibility that it was not an entire fabrication though at first blush there was not much inherent probability in all the spoof he got off his chest being strictly accurate gospel' (16.826–9). Bloom speaks of 'positive forgeries' (16.781) and he himself may be one; it is also possible that the convoluted expression in the sentence just quoted, like the whole discourse of 'Eumaeus', is an instance of Joyce having fun at the expense of 'proper English', playing with the inherent potential for deformations in the nature of language. In this way the chapter's style is part and parcel of Joyce's assault on the conventions of English while also allowing for displays of his habitual humour – as when Bloom counsels Stephen against trusting Mulligan 'if I were in your shoes' (16.281), not knowing that Stephen is wearing Mulligan's cast-off shoes, adding for good measure that Mulligan 'knows which side his bread is buttered' without the knowledge that he butters his bread on both sides (1.447). Language is elusive, not as easy to ground itself in certainty as some would wish for, and Joyce enjoys flouting its lack of prescriptive rules.

The episode's ending, with Bloom and Stephen conversing as they make their way 'side by side' to Eccles St (16.1880), does not sentimentalize their relationship; the differences between them are made clear but the words in italics are from a song, 'The Low-Backed Car', that celebrates a marriage. The idea of some kind of union of opposites is developed in the next episode.

ITHACA

Time

1–2 a.m.

Place

7 Eccles St

Plot

Bloom has forgotten his keys and climbs over railings and drops down to an area that accesses his kitchen, going upstairs with a candle to open the front door for the waiting Stephen. Bloom makes cocoa for both of them and, spotting two torn betting tickets on the dresser, realizes they were Boylan's bets on the Gold Cup race and that he had unknowingly given Bantam Lyons the name Throwaway, the winning horse. In conversation, Stephen recites some Irish verse and Bloom some Hebrew from the Song of Songs; the different languages and races are compared before Stephen chants an anti-semitic ballad about a ritual killing. Bloom thinks of his daughter before suggesting Stephen spend the night in his house. The invitation is declined but they agree to meet again. Leaving through the back door, they observe the clear night sky in the garden and Bloom reflects on aspects of the heavenly bodies. They both urinate, looking up at the lighted bedroom window where Molly lies. After shaking hands, Stephen departs from Bloom and from the book, destination unknown. Bloom returns indoors and upstairs to a living room where he finds the furniture rearranged. Sitting at a table, his day's budget is supplied, omitting the train fare to the brothel area and the money paid there, and he contemplates an ideal lifestyle in his dream house. He places his letter from Martha Clifford in one of two locked drawers, the other one contains financial and personal documents and includes his father's suicide note. Thinking of his life, Bloom contemplates departure to a new location and sees himself as a wanderer among the stars before reviewing the day's events and making his way into the bedroom. Undressing, his gets into bed and lays his head at the end opposite to Molly and feels the impression left there by Boylan before resolving his feelings about what has happened there earlier in the day. His kissing of Molly's bottom awakens her sufficiently to listen to his account of the day before he drifts off to sleep, dreaming of Sinbad the Sailor.

Discussion

The apparently 'unliterary' style of 'Ithaca', different again from anything that has gone before, adopts what appears to be a rigidly scientific and objective account of what takes place between Bloom and Stephen in the early hours of 17 June 1904. Joyce wrote to Budgen:

> I am writing Ithaca in the form of a mathematical equation. All events are resolved into their cosmic, physical, etc equivalents . . . so that the reader will know everything and know it in the baldest and coldest way, but Bloom and Stephen thereby become heavenly bodies, wanderers like the stars at which they gaze.[43]

True to Joyce's word, the deadpan catechism in 'Ithaca' yields a goldmine of information about Bloom, not just data regarding his age, height, weight and the contents of his bookshelf but facts about the absence of sexual intercourse in his marriage since before Rudy's birth, over ten years ago. The encyclopaedic style of 'Eumaeus', despite the valuable information released, obeys an impersonal logic and applies itself indiscriminately, as in the absurd comparison between the patterns of urination belonging to Bloom and Stephen (17.1192–8), the 450-word answer to a question about Bloom and water (17.185–228) or the excess technical jargon floating around in the unlocking of the back gate (17.1215–9). Joyce's humour is still keenly at work, allowing the particular style of an episode to follow its own logic and stray outside the fictional narrative.

What is remarkable is the way the poignant humanity of Bloom and Stephen emerges through, or despite, the clinical and apparently disinterested prose of the narrator. On the face of it, there is little to suggest that either Bloom or Stephen have been changed by their coming together – 'Given that their communion is based on drinking cocoa and urinating together, should we wonder whether their relationship and its significance may prove ephemeral?'[44] – and the singing of the anti-semitic 'Little Harry Hughes' (17.802–28) indicates not bigotry but Stephen's absorption in himself as victim, the price he sees himself paying for being an artist. Yet Joyce's cosmic frame of reference places both individuals in a context that brings them together as lonely, isolated bodies in time and space dwarfed by the 'drift of socalled fixed stars, in reality evermoving wanderers from immeasurably remote eons to infinitely remote futures in comparison with which the years, threescore and ten, of allotted human life formed a parenthesis of infinitesimal brevity' (17.1052–6). The brevity of life informs the mutual awareness of death that accompanies their final parting to the sound of nearby church bells, making the leave-taking a moment of solidarity: Stephen thinks of the prayer for the dying and his mother and Bloom recalls the morning's ringing that brought the deceased Paddy Dignam to his mind (17.1230–4). They separate and go their own ways but Bloom, who sees in Stephen 'the predestination of a future' (17.780), knows the 'accent of the ecstasy of catastrophe' (17.786) and fatalistically accepts time, change and the unavoidable potential for unhappiness. The moment of solidarity was all too brief and with Stephen's departure Bloom is left with existential dread, feeling 'the cold of interstellar space' (17.1246) in an indifferent universe.

Metaphor and philosophy emerge out of the chapter's relentless empiricism and nowhere more so than in the lyrical response to the scientific inquiry as to what awaited them when stepping out into the back garden: 'The heaventree of stars hung with humid nightblue fruit' (17.1039). Such a poetic utterance is later disqualified (17.1139–44), but only putatively for the reader because it has a place in the evocation of a cosmic dimension where Bloom and Stephen are two 'heavenly bodies' following 'parallel courses' (17.1). There is no merging of minds but there is companionship and some brief degree of fellowship as well as the picture of their wandering lives moving through space and time, following patterns they themselves are rarely aware of. The part of the body that Joyce associated with 'Ithaca' in the Gilbert and Linati schemas is the skeleton and this somatic correspondence befits a chapter resonant with reminders of the finitude of human existence.

The style of this chapter also transcends the limitations it might be expected to pose for dealing with a correspondence between heroic Odysseus slaying the suitors in Ithaca and Bloom's conquest when he returns home. That there are correspondences is clear enough: Odysseus enters his house indirectly, as does Bloom his; the throwing of a stool at him by an angry suitor has a parallel in Bloom's collision with a piece of displaced furniture in his room; Stephen 'helped to close and chain the door' (17.119) just as Telemachus does for Odysseus; and after the slaughter Odysseus fumigates his house, as does Bloom (17.1321–9). Bloom's slaying of Boylan is an unepic triumph of the mind over circumstances, a process of amelioration whereby nominatives chart a movement from wrath through denial to acceptance without rancour: 'Envy, jealousy, abnegation, equanimity' (17.2155) pass through his mind when thinking of Molly's adultery. The end of this episode, the end of Bloom's day, comes to rest with a large dot or period – Joyce instructed the printers to enlarge it – as if objective language has reached its limit in communicating the truths behind one man's odyssey through Dublin on a particular day in June 1904. Methodological imperatives are swamped by a slippery salaciousness when describing Bloom's kissing of Molly's bottom: 'He kissed the plump mellow yellow smellow melons of her rump, on each plump melonous hemisphere, in their mellow yellow furrow, with obscure prolonged provocative melonsmellonous osculation' (17.2241–3). The cataloguing principle that has dominated the style breaks down as Bloom drifts into sleep thinking of 'Sinbad the Sailor and Tinbad the Tailor and Jinbad the Jailer . . . Linbad the Yailer and Xinbad the Phthailer' (17.2322–6), collapsing itself in a meaningless iteration without even the comfort of alliteration. As one critic finely observed of the episode's concluding language: 'The technique, the novel itself, has fallen to sleep with Bloom.'[45]

Bloom's 'equanimity' is partly rendered in an acceptance of his Jewishness, an issue that has been worrying away at his self-esteem during the course of the day. Conversing together in Eccles Street, Bloom and Stephen do not openly allude to their difference but the nature of Bloom's Jewishness is in both their minds and they share a sense of how notions of being Irish or Jewish are tangled affairs involving myths, religion, nationalism and economic power. Bloom sings a Hebrew lyric about hope and return and, after Stephen's departure, burns the Zionist *Agendath Netaim* prospectus picked up in the butcher's shop at the start of his day. He comes to see that Judaism is no less rational than other religions (17.1902–3), feels 'remorse' (17.1893) for disrespecting his father's beliefs and remembers his journeying across Europe as a persecuted Jew (17.1905–15).

PENELOPE

Time

Early hours of the morning

Place

7 Eccles St

Plot

In the first 'sentence' (18.1–245) Molly begins with surprise at thinking Bloom has requested breakfast in bed and wonders with suspicion about his whereabouts that night. She has seen him writing secretively and suspects there is another woman involved, bringing to mind her dismissal of a maidservant who might have been attracting her husband's attention (and pilfering oysters from the household). Bloom's tendency to enjoy the idea of Molly desiring another man leads her to dwell on sexuality and Boylan. Bloom's mention of seeing Mrs Breen reminds Molly of how they all knew one another in years past.

Molly's concern over Boylan occupies much of the second sentence (18.246–534) and she is impatient for her next meeting with him on Monday and the concert tour to Belfast the following week. She thinks of her early life in Gibraltar and its British army background as well as Stanley Gardner, a soldier who had died. She dwells on Bloom's inadequacies, the need for some money for new clothes and how she had intervened to no effect when Bloom lost his job at a cattle merchant's business. Molly's sexual awareness, if not hunger, is the concern of the next sentence (18.535–95).

Molly recalls her life in Gibraltar in the fourth sentence (18.596–747) and remembering the sad parting from her friend Hester Stanhope and her attractive husband only accentuates her present state of boredom. She longs for a letter, admitting that Boylan is more coarse than romantic, something to enliven the days before she grows old. The fifth sentence (18.748–908) concerns the letter she received from Harry Mulvey, a soldier based in Gibraltar and her first real lover. She recalls the romance, the excitement and her sense of superiority over other Dublin female singers. She breaks wind.

The sixth sentence (18.909–1148) brings Bloom back into her mind and she thinks affectionately of his morning routine, his hopelessness at rowing and her relationship with Milly. She feels her period coming on and gets out of the bed to sit on a chamber pot. A change in Molly's attitude towards Bloom emerges in the seventh sentence (18.1149–367) as she recalls how his letters produced such sexual excitement in her. She laughs at his odd ways, like sleeping upside-down in bed, but as she gets back into bed herself she worries over their financial insecurity and his ability to keep a job. Annoyed that Bloom might have been with a woman, she determines to search his pockets in the morning and wonders about his male friends like Simon Dedlaus. This causes her to wonder about Stephen and what Bloom has in mind, responding warmly to the idea of a sexual liaison with a distinguished, educated young poet.

Molly's sexual imagination continues into the last sentence (18.1368–609), with Boylan's allure diminishing and blame thrown onto Bloom for not responding to her desires. Caring thoughts about the young Stephen bring uncomfortable memories about Rudy to mind and she imagines Stephen as a lodger in their house. Molly seeks to reclaim Bloom, planning special efforts to gain his attention, admitting her adultery and accommodating his liking for ejaculating over her bottom while obtaining from him a modest sum of money. Before falling asleep, her thoughts about Bloom fuse with a sweet

memory of time with Mulvey in Gibraltar as she affirms joyously the
moment on Howth Head with Bloom.

Discussion

Molly is traditionally viewed as the embodiment of womanhood and
'Penelope' often read as a flowing discourse emanating from the
female body, manifesting the physicality and libidinousness from
which subjectivity emerges, a representation of human drives that
Joyce spoke of as being at the materialist heart of literature: 'The
modern theme is the subterranean forces, those hidden tides which
govern everything and run humanity counter to the apparent flood;
those poisonous subtleties which envelop the soul, the ascending
fumes of sex.'[46] The voice of Molly as a fluid form of the body and
its demands requires a style of expression utterly different to the
exhaustive locutions of 'Ithaca'. The psychic space for qualification,
reflection or circumlocution does not exist, this is the unstanched
voice of the flesh, the female sex affirming desire, and for some feminist critics this causes concern: 'thinking and menstruating are similar
and concomitant processes. She can no more govern the first, by
sentence structure or punctuation, than she can the second.'[47] This
notion of 'Penelope' as a free-flowing, haemorrhaging of uncensored
consciousness – a conception that resurrects the tired dichotomy
of male logos and female irrationality – ignores its rule-governed
adherence to sentence structure; hence the ability of one editor, Danis
Rose, to assign it punctuation unproblematically (Joyce removed
much of the punctuation at a late proof stage). Unlike Bloom's interior monologues, often fuelled by the random nature of stimuli on
the street, Molly is following a train of thoughts in her mind and,
as the reader soon discovers, it is not difficult to sense where one
thought ends and another begins. She may lack the convention of
punctuation (the ancient Greeks, who also wrote without punctuation, did without interword spacing as well) but generously bestows
proper nouns for places, especially places with sexual associations.
Molly tends to discard people's names, those of males particularly,
and in a characteristic sentence like 'I liked the way he made
love then . . . but he never knew how to embrace well like Gardner
I hope hell come on Monday' (18.328–32) she promiscuously favours
the pronoun, with the first 'he' referring to Bloom and the second

to Boylan. What occupies Molly as signifiers of the meaningful are place names, clothes, body parts, bodily functions, unguents. Boylan's straw hat features more than once as a prop supporting the self-image of a debonair young man (6.199, 8.1168, 11.302) but it is a straw hat worn by Bloom (18.1573) that comes to Molly in the episode's climax.

The reservations of some feminist critics are broadly overcome by a consensus that the gender-challenged author has managed something quite unique with Molly Bloom. In myth, Penelope unravels her day's work during the night as her stratagem for dealing with the insistent suitors, nightly undoing her promise to marry one of them when she has finished weaving what she says will be a shroud for the father of Odysseus. Molly's soliloquy can be seen as an unweaving of her attachment to Boylan, without abandoning her right to sexual enjoyment, rising to a breathless crescendo that reaffirms her union with Bloom. She slays the suitors by thinking of and preferring Bloom and his eccentricities to Boylan's 'determined vicious look' (18.153) that made her half close her eyes during their sex. She looks forward to his next visit on Monday and the trip to Belfast with him but her final, altitudinous thoughts concern Bloom. Leopold, she recalls, wrote 'mad crazy letters' (18.1176) that made her want to masturbate repeatedly and he gave her a present of Byron's poems; Boylan, by comparison, exists in a poor light: 'no manners nor no refinement . . . the ignoramus that doesnt know poetry from a cabbage' (18.1368–71) and cannot write a good letter. Molly responds to poetry and letters because it is words that hold out a dream for her – a dream that she fears is slipping into the past -- and her poetic sensibility finds expression in the language of planting and flowering.[48]

There is another side to Molly Bloom, less an earth mother than a housewife in a home without an indoor toilet, coping with the quotidian, planning meals (18.939–45). She likes music, song and military parades, reads popular literature of the day and takes a canny pride in her appearance. She is a woman in history, the daughter of a British soldier, Major Brian Tweedy, brought up in the British colony of Gibraltar and its expatriate military community until about the age of sixteen. Her mother, Lunita Laredo, either left home or died when she was young. Mrs Bloom has no time for Irish nationalism, disliking the anti-British politics associated with the Boer War and preferring to link Bloemfontein not with a battle but with the memory of a boyfriend who died there of a fever while on duty. Her life-affirming energy triumphs over the politics and, remembering how when she was pregnant Bloom wanted to use her milk in his tea, Molly can be seen as a modern replacement for the milkwoman of 'Telemachus' as an emblem of Ireland.

The human side to her married life in 1904 Dublin is not idealized or sentimentalized and as Declan Kiberd observes, Bloom

> never does manage to put his arms around his wife and forgive her in person, as he has already forgiven her in his mind; and she never tells him what she has already told herself, that he is still the finest man in Dublin and handsome to boot.[49]

Molly as a complex individual in her own right risks losing her place when interpretations situate her as part of the chapter's dynamic which, in Joyce's own words, 'turns like the huge earth ball, slowly surely evenly round and round spinning, its four cardinal points being the female breasts, arse, womb and cunt expressed by the words *because, bottom . . . woman, yes.*'[50] The symbolism is very open to interpretation because it is not clear, unlike the earthy voice of Molly herself. Many readers have heard and recognised the bona fide voices of male Dubliners in the bar scenes of *Ulysses*; equally authentic is the female voice of Molly, vain but class-conscious and subversive in its hedonism, as in the passage where she gustily denigrates would-be cultural nationalists:

> Kathleen Kearney and her lot of squealers Miss This Miss That Miss Theother lot of sparrowfarts skitting around talking about politics they know as much about as my backside anything in the world to make themselves someway interesting Irish homemade beauties soldiers daughter am I ay and whose are you bootmakers and publicans I beg your pardon coach I thought you were a wheelbarrow theyd die down dead off their feet if they ever got the chance of walking down the Alameda on an officers arm like me on the bandnight. (18.878–85)[51]

Passages any longer than this are not likely to continue for long without revealing some information about the sex lives of Molly and Leopold. Fetishes, fantasies, masturbation, oral sex and transgressions circulate freely, unabashed and unashamed. 'At first I had not thought of the slaughter of the suitors as in Ulysses' character. Now I see it can be there too. I am going to leave the last word with

Molly Bloom', [52] wrote Joyce to Frank Budgen on 10 December 1920, and in her affirmation of desire and superb awareness of the body's social semiotics she becomes, as Colin MacCabe put it, 'the destroyer of the phallic pretensions'.[53] Lenehan, with his macho account in 'Wandering Rocks' of sitting next to Molly in a coach ride (10.566–74), is dismissed as quickly as one of the suitors shot by Ulysses with his bow: 'that sponger he was making free of me after the Glencree dinner' and Molly thinks more of the delicious chicken she enjoyed at the meal (18.426–32). Her enjoyment of the food is one part of her great affirmation, 'Yes', that is repeated so many times in her soliloquy – a repetition that caused difficulty for translators of the novel into Irish in 1991, since there is no simple Irish word for yes or for no. Molly Bloom, though, shares with her husband vital non-Irish characteristics. She was born in Gibraltar, the daughter of Major Brian Tweedy and his Spanish-Jewish wife Lunita Laredo.

CHAPTER 4

CRITICAL RECEPTION AND
PUBLISHING HISTORY

The publication history of *Ulysses* is a narrative in its own right and an ongoing one.[1] As the novel neared completion it became clear to Joyce that finding a publisher would not be an easy matter. Fortune intervened in the figure of Sylvia Beach (1887–1962), an American-born bookseller in Paris whose bookshop became a meeting place for the city's expatriate literary intellectuals. She made an offer to publish the book in 1921 and also found a printer in Dijon who was happy to provide galley proofs for checking. This was an open cheque to Joyce to revise and add further text, a process that went on almost to the day *Ulysses* was published, on the author's fortieth birthday 2 February 1922, its covers appropriately enshrined in the blue-and-white colours of Greece.

T. S. ELIOT'S *ULYSSES*

T. S. Eliot's influential essay '*Ulysses*, Order and Myth', which first appeared towards the end of 1923, hailed Joyce's novel as a seminal work of the century and his mythical method, the use of Homeric correspondences, as having 'the importance of a scientific discovery. No one else has built a novel upon such a foundation before: it has never before been necessary.'[2] For Eliot, the way now lay open for a radical development that would alter the course of twentieth-century literature: 'In using myth, in manipulating a continuous parallel between contemporaneity and antiquity, Mr Joyce is pursuing a method which others must pursue after him.' Joyce's new method is important not only for the future course of literature but for any

87

epistemological claim that modern art might wish to make: 'It is simply a way of controlling, of ordering, of giving a shape and significance to the immense panorama of futility and anarchy which is contemporary history.' The form of the novel before *Ulysses* is seen as 'the expression of an age': the nineteenth-century novel was a form in the sense that what is seen to be essential and unique about the structural organization and writing of a novel of that period is an expression of what is also essential and unique, although in a different non-literary way, about nineteenth-century society and culture. *Ulysses*, while possessing certain superficial features in common with the form of a novel is not really a novel in the sense that it does not, and cannot, possess this organic sense of form. The *a priori* harmony that could exist between the form of the novel and the form of the society that produced such novels is a phenomenon that, regrettably for Eliot, comes to an end with the modern world; a structural change in society necessitates an alteration in literary form and Joyce's importance is that he is in the vanguard of this momentous change.

Underlying Eliot's interpretation is an unstated realist aesthetic that relates causally the world of events to the world of the novel; a connection that transcends the merely phenomenal and gives rise to an underlying representationalism that allows Eliot to state that the novel 'was simply the expression of an age which had not sufficiently lost all form to feel the need of something stricter.' The term 'simply' is here referring not to something artless or naïve but rather an unforced representation of what already existed in the social organism. With the twentieth century, however, a crisis has arisen – 'the novel ended with Flaubert and with James' – and it follows that the cause of this crisis is not to be located within the literary sphere but within the broader cultural and social order that produced the novel. A change in the social order involves the withering away of the novel as a useful means of expression and, because the 'novel is a form which will no longer serve', the narrative method is to be superseded by the mythical method. The mythical method, however, does not entail a similar kind of representationalism because it does not emerge from the social order in the same way that the nineteenth-century novel did and therefore does not seem to possess the same ontological truth as the narrative method. The social order is a 'panorama of futility' and the role of literature is a kind of policing one; culture becoming an order imposed on the anarchy of history and rendering a set of values in the process.

The hierarchical relationship Eliot establishes between Homer's mythical world and that of Dublin in 1904 is not as obvious as Eliot takes it to be and in one way his essay reveals more about *The Waste Land* than it does about *Ulysses*. As an example, take the passage in 'Calypso' describing the start of Bloom's walk from his house to the butcher's shop (4.77–99). Here there is no hierarchy between the Orient and Dublin; instead, one merges into the other and then back again, as with the interaction of colour common to both ('Night sky, moon, violet, colour of Molly's new garters.') or the colloquialisms ('Dander along all day.'). Bloom knows he is imagining a stereotyped view of the East: 'Turbaned faces going by. Dark caves of carpet shops, big man, Turko the terrible, seating crosslegged smoking a coiled pipe . . . . Probably not a bit like it really. Kind of stuff you read'. Comparing this with, say, the description of the typist in *The Waste Land* one sees how in Eliot's poem other material is used to create and sustain an ethical viewpoint; any such tendentiousness is absent from the Joyce passage.

MODERNIST *ULYSSES*

Another important critic in the early reception of *Ulysses* is Ezra Pound. European modernism was promoted by Pound as an avant-garde movement of literary innovators pursuing a radical aesthetic that would regenerate the declining cultural health of society; and Joyce was hailed as a cardinal figure and fellow founding member of this movement. Language for Pound had been conscripted into the service of convention and tradition as purveyor of falsification but the 'metallic exactitude' of Joyce's writing is praised for its debunking aesthetic: 'The valid parallels for *Ulysses* are with Cerventes chewing up the Spanish Romances and with Rabelais chewing up scholastic bunk, and the idolatry of written words in his own day.'[3] Such praise was based on his reading of the early chapters as they appeared in instalments but by the time of the 'Sirens' chapter doubts emerged about the change in style: 'subject good enough to hold attention without being so all bloodily fricasseed.'[4] Such reservations proved to be the genesis of a growing estrangement but, while he had little time for what Joyce went on to write, Pound helped establish the status of *Ulysses* as the canonical modernist text; and not least because it steered away from the ideological preoccupations of Pound. Joyce's novel was greeted as internationalist in spirit, disavowing a narrow-gauge nationalism and championing cosmopolitanism.

Joyce himself played a managerial and hands-on role in the promotion of his novel by sanctioning two works of exegesis written by close acquaintances. The first of these was Stuart Gilbert's *James Joyce's Ulysses*, published in 1930 and written in the conscious knowledge that although the novel's fame had been established its readership in English-speaking countries was curtailed by the publishing bans in force at the time. Before the whole novel appeared in 1922 various parts of it had been published in magazines: Harriet Shaw Weaver's *The Egoist* brought five episodes to public attention in 1919 and around the same time parts also appeared in *The Little Review*, an American magazine devoted to avant-garde art. Anticipating official reactions to the novel's 1922 publication, *The Little Review* was charged with obscenity, fined and forbidden to publish any further episodes. At the end of 1922, Customs impounded a copy being brought into Britain and it was subsequently banned. A shipment of 500 copies was seized at a port on the south coast and destroyed early the following year and in 1926 it came to the notice of the authorities that an academic at Cambridge University, F. R. Leavis, had ordered a copy through a bookseller and was proposing to lecture on it. The Director of Public Prosecutions alerted the Chancellor of the university and the planned lectures were cancelled. A ban was not necessary in Ireland because no bookseller would dare stock a copy.

Stuart Gilbert's guide circumvented the bans by including lengthy quotations from the text and he kept them in for the revised edition in 1952 even though by then copies could readily be obtained. In 1933 a judge in the US had declared it fit for publication – concluding that although its effect on readers is often 'somewhat emetic, nowhere does it tend to be aphrodisiac'[5] – and Random House brought out an edition in 1934. Joyce was world famous by this time, appearing on the front cover of *Time* magazine at the time of its first American edition, and The Bodley Head in London decided to test the water and publish 1,000 copies in 1936. Though officially banned, the authorities decided to take no action. Gilbert's guide draws heavily on the *Odyssey* and it is hard to avoid thinking that Joyce was laying down Homeric lights on the runway preparing the way for the descent of academia. The second book that Joyce sanctioned was Frank Budgen's *James Joyce and the Making of Ulysses*, published in 1934.

This too was a collaborative effort in some ways, with Joyce compiling sheets of suggestions for Budgen's consideration.

An independent study of *Ulysses* was published in 1932 by Edmund Wilson in his *Axel's Castle*; an essay which was one of the first sustained attempts to harmonize the practice of *Ulysses* with a theory of realism. He admits to a sense of frustration which he attributes to an excess of design in some of the Homeric parallels and struggles to come to terms with the stylistic adventures in the later chapters but he praises Joyce for achieving something new in literature: 'showing us the world as his characters perceive it, to find the unique vocabulary and rhythm which will represent the thoughts of each.'[6] Joyce's intention is to capture the fullness and totality of a city's life in the twentieth century and this cannot be achieved by simply imitating the form of the novel from the previous century. Wilson, echoing Eliot, compares Joyce's world with Einstein's – a shifting phenomenon that in essence is composed of an infinite number of events – and the form for mirroring this must abandon the staple ingredients of the novel of the past and adopt techniques that will allow the artist to capture the multidimensional space–time continuum of twentieth-century life and thought.

THE AMERICAN *ULYSSES*

The canonical status that *Ulysses* was acquiring was enhanced by the work of the American critic Richard Ellmann when he published an enormously influential biography of Joyce in 1959, subsequently revised for a new edition in 1982, presenting the writer as a rarefied, apolitical artist. Three studies published in the 1970s showed the continuing influence of the idea that a schema could unlock *Ulysses*. Ellmann himself brought out a study in 1972 based around a dialectical, triadic structure (see pages 40–41): 'One symmetry required another: if one chapter is external, the next is internal, and the third a mixture . . . if one is solar, the second will be lunar, and the third will envisage an alchemical marriage of sun and moon.'[7] Joyce read the work of Victor Bérard (1863–1931), a classical scholar who linked Odysseus's journeys with Mediterranean trade routes, and another study, Seidel's *Epic Geography*, traced a geographical pattern within *Ulysses* that was seen to consciously emulate the spatial orientations of the ancient Greek epic. For Marilyn French in *The Book as World*, Dante provides the model for the structure of *Ulysses* and French read the novel in terms of a series of circles 'not of states of damnation or salvation, but of perception . . . the varying distances are Joyce's equivalent to Dante's moral hierarchy' and the reader voyages in and out of these circles.[8]

These three critics were all American and so also was Hugh Kenner, the most noted Joyce scholar of this period apart from Ellmann. Kenner gave gravitas and grace to what by now was a well-oiled Joyce industry by taking up Ezra Pound's positioning of the author within High Modernism and claiming him as a great artist of the modern world. Kenner's first book on Joyce appeared in 1956, *Dublin's Joyce*, with heuristic-sounding chapter titles like 'How to Read *Ulysses*' and 'The Plan of *Ulysses*', and this was followed by a full-length study of the novel in 1980. Before the advent of theory in the late 1970s, it was his shorter *Joyce's Voices*, published in 1978, that most successfully handled the stylistic excursions in *Ulysses* without abandoning a humanist approach to the novel. Kenner posits a principle of Joyce's writing whereby what one takes to be a narrative voice is in fact a verbal pose that reflects a character in that part of the book. He gives examples to show how the style of the first half of 'Nausicaa' is best viewed as the voice of Gerty MacDowell intermingling with and helping to produce the narrative drive of the chapter. In this sentence, for instance, one can see what Kenner calls the Uncle Charles principle – 'the narrative idiom need not be the narrator's'[9] – at work: 'There was an innate refinement, a languid queenly *hauteur* about Gerty which was unmistakably evidenced in her delicate hands and higharched instep.' (13.96–8). It is not that Gerty uses these words to describe herself but the style reflects how she would like to be described. Similarly, when Boylan is in a flower shop sending a gift to Molly the reader encounters Boylan-verbs (italics added): 'The blond girl in Thornton's *bedded* the wicker basket' (10.299); and Boylan-epithets: 'She bestowed fat pears neatly, head by tail, and among them *ripe shamefaced* peaches' (10.305–6). Later on when Bloom returns home he notices 'an oval wicker basket *bedded* with fibre and containing one Jersey pear' and 'a halfempty bottle of William Gilbey and Co's white invalid port, half *disrobed* of its swathe of coralpink tissue paper' (17.304–7). Boylan's presence in Bloom's mind is signified in the language.

It is interesting to see how Kenner handled aspects of *Ulysses* that around this time, the late 1970s, were beginning to attract European theorists for very different reasons. While the style of 'Eumaeus', one of those 'difficult' chapters that seem to frustrate the pleasures of reading narrative fiction, is seen as the voice of a narrator being Bloom as he would like to see himself – urbane, educated and mannerly – Kenner does detect a significant change in the styles of *Ulysses* with the 'Sirens' episode, a chapter that sets up 'screens of language'[10] between the reader and the story. The story itself is approaching the hour when Boylan and Molly will meet but the narrative is subordinated to an exercise in style and the fugue-like opening is 'as though, to amuse us while Agamemnon dies, a magician were to attempt the levitation of Cassandra, absorbing the full attention of the Chorus.'[11] For Kenner, such stylistic diversions are characteristic of the last two-thirds of *Ulysses*; a quite deliberate attempt to conceal the events that are hidden behind the language. It is an expression of the Irish cult of nostalgia that Bloom allows himself to be distracted by the musical banalities and sad clichés of this chapter; a polemical use of the past that betrays character rather than offering any genuine evocation of past history. Joyce is seen to be fascinated with the way people play out their roles and alter them by a change in diction and costume and, though allied to Shakespeare in this respect, it is also seen as characteristic of a race whose 'Irish eyes will challenge us to produce a subject that exists apart from the words.'[12] It leads to a philosophical distrust of ideas in favour of pure style and Joyce is seen as writing a work committed to the principle that reality is a matter of style, an expression of an alleged racial trait whereby the Irish are just infatuated with their own voices. Kenner postulates a devious second narrator, Irish by nature, wholly committed to the Uncle Charles principle, who grows in power as the novel progresses. The multiple styles, reflecting the varied voices of Dublin gossip, gradually proliferate and dominate the book.

POST-STRUCTURALIST *ULYSSES*

It seemed that American academics had a monopoly on post-World War II Joyce scholarship and when in 1967 the James Joyce Foundation was set up to promote international scholarship two of the three founders were American (the third, Fritz Senn, was Swiss). Change was in the air, however, and it was at the 1975 Joyce Symposium in Paris that a set of critical practices, now loosely known as 'theory', were introduced to a wider audience and came to be seen as part of what became known as post-structuralism. In the late 1960s and early 1970s essays began appearing in the French avant-garde journal *Tel Quel* championing Joyce as one of the radical figures who questioned the nature of language. Intellectuals like Jacques Lacan, Hélène Cixous and Jacques Derrida, addressing issues of narrative and style, began to refer to Joyce and even emulate him in their own complex, dense and punning ways of writing. The apparent transparency of language as a system locked into the structure of an objective reality was rejected and replaced by new accounts of the slippery signifier floating in a linguistic space and constitutive of reality rather than reflecting it. The valorization of *Ulysses* as a realist work of fiction had now passed its meridian and critics came to applaud instead the self-referentiality of its writing and its shift away from the notion of a unified point of view, the 'meaning' of a novel, in favour of a more 'open' text that foregrounds its own medium and in the process interrogates its own practice of novel writing.

In 1972 a prescient article by Stephen Heath appeared in *Tel Quel* and though concentrating on *Finnegans Wake* the essay draws on all Joyce's writings in order to establish a case for re-evaluating him in the light of 'strategies of hesitancy'[13], a term referring to those aspects of the writing that interrupt any attempt to impose upon the author classical notions of 'continuity', 'meaning' and 'style'. It is claimed that style, understood as the characteristic 'voice' of the author, cannot be found in Joyce, as evidenced by the difficulty of attempts to parody him. To parody an author is to isolate and imitate those individualized features of a writer that the reader comes to recognize as characteristic; with Joyce there exists the problem of knowing where to look for the style among a multiplicity of styles that feed off all previous manners and modes of writing. The source of such a negation of style is located by Heath in the endeavour to escape the 'paralysis' that Joyce identified at the heart of Dublin[14] by skirting the very terms that fix a sense for the act of reading, liberating himself and the reader by continually evading sense through a play with form; hence the impossibility of employing the notion of metaphor to Joyce:

> in so far as that writing deconstructs the fundamental (contextual) distinction between the literal and the figurative: according to what criteria are any particular elements to be identified as metaphors

in a text in which every element refers to another, perpetually deferring meaning.[15]

Opposing the theoretical foundations to realist accounts of *Ulysses*, post-structuralism suggests that language is a system with an excessive flow of signifiers over signifieds and the linguistic rules that govern our written and oral communication are not ultimately derived from some exterior reality that is supposed to give credence to the language but are purely and simply rules: arbitrary conventions that produce rather than express meanings. The post-structuralist critic welcomed the 'unreadability' of parts of *Ulysses* and claimed that what is at stake here is the mechanism of producing multiple meanings.

Such an approach remained largely confined to the Continent until in 1979 English-speaking readers were introduced to this new Joyce with the publication of Colin MacCabe's *James Joyce & the Revolution of the Word*. The title refers to an essay by F. R. Leavis[16] in which Joyce's work is identified as broadly symptomatic of an uprooted and alienated society. A literary practice that Leavis rejected as being unhealthy and restrictive, dried up from the linguistic wellspring of any real community, is now hailed by MacCabe as an energizing assault on the unhealthy and restrictive act of passively consuming literature. The text is seen to counteract any attempt to become immersed in the story; and the expectations that the reader may harbour for a universal process of development, revelation and cathartic epilogue is sabotaged by a writing that explodes the myth that the objects of mimesis can be separated from the set of discourses articulated by the text. Lacan is evoked to show how entry into the symbolic world of language necessarily involves a painful loss of being as it denies the possible existence of a stable, unified subject. All that is possible is a series of subject positions that language makes available; positions that are seen as inherently antithetical to the chance of conferring any lasting identity. This is seen to be the case because of the nature of post-Saussurean linguistics which postulates language as a system built upon internal and arbitrary differences that have no epistemological value other than the internal logic of the linguistic system. Such internal relationships offer only the appearance of a fixity because of the forceful needs of the human ego which struggles for a rooted and homogenous identity.

Post-structuralism and deconstruction became passé in the 1980s and quickly fed into the North American Joyce industry. The first self-consciously post-structuralist readings of Joyce were given at the 1982 International James Joyce Symposium and by the time of the next symposium in Frankfurt, two years later, such readings were the norm and Derrida gave an address. Books like Karen Lawrence's *The Odyssey of Styles in Ulysses* made the almost obligatory assault on the possibility of a 'meaning' being found in the pages of Joyce's novel: 'We see the styles as different but not definite ways of filtering and ordering experience. This view of styles obviates a "spatial apprehension" of the book; one cannot see through the various styles to an ultimate Platonic pattern of meaning.'[17] The Homeric journey, the search for home and a reaffirmation of identity came to be seen purely in terms of language and the different chapters were read as adventures into a literary form or a particular discourse that offered the prospect of the subject finding itself. This quest leads to no conclusion, there is no linguistic Ithaca to which the reader can return and find the certitude of a unified subject. What is left after Joyce's versatile depletion of styles exposes the linguistic and literary wrack that we call language? Is it just sounds, as when Stephen closed his eyes in 'Proteus' 'to hear his boots crush crackling wrack and shells' (3.10)? The result of exclusively merging *Ulysses* with theories of language can be to locate the novel within an historical vacuum, hermetically sealed off from its social and political context, creating a timelessness that contributes to a reification of language. An obsession with the sheer materiality of language can finally have the result of de-materializing reality, although for MacCabe there was a politics to the realization that any one subject position is constructed by and through a particular discourse. Joyce was partnered with Lenin because texts like *Ulysses* are 'revolutionary in their commitment to the overthrow of the possibility of contemporary (both his and ours) political discourse.'[18] MacCabe's logic is suspect because the transition from Lenin to Joyce cannot be implemented by just asserting that they both oppose and destroy an existing paradigm – a deconstruction within the literary sphere does not necessarily entail any questioning of the political status quo – although MacCabe did show how Joyce's political understanding was far more knowledgeable and sustained than the one anchored in traditional views of him as a quintessentially mandarin writer. It was not until the advent of post-colonialist studies, that a more fertile way emerged of reading *Ulysses* as the work of a politically engaged writer.

POST-COLONIALIST *ULYSSES*

Stephen's conversation with the English Dean of Studies at university in *A Portrait of the Artist as a Young Man* provides the seminal statement for a post-colonialist reading of Joyce:

> How different are the words *home, Christ, ale, master*, on his lips and on mine! . . . . His language, so familiar and so foreign, will always be for me an acquired speech. I have not made or accepted such words. My voice holds them at bay.[19]

As a theoretical approach to literature, post-colonialism is not without conceptual difficulties and as a way of interpreting Irish texts it is a contentious field. Notwithstanding, it seems clear that Joyce's writing is bound up with the political state of Ireland as he saw it; and it is from just such a perspective that some of the best literary criticism in relation to *Ulysses* has appeared over the last two decades. The process of re-reading Joyce in relation to the specific historical and cultural context for *Ulysses*, that of Ireland as a colonial state under British rule, began in the 1980s with work by important Irish scholars.[20] This was followed in the 1990s by books such as David Lloyd's *Anomalous States: Irish Writing and the Post-Colonial Moment* (1993), Enda Duffy's *The Subaltern Ulysses* (1994), Emer Nolan's *James Joyce and Nationalism* (1995) and Vincent Cheng's *Joyce, Race and Empire* (1995). Nolan questions the simplistic view of Joyce as the quintessential metropolitan who in the spirit of international modernism divorced himself from outmoded concepts like nationalism. Cheng's study shows how racial and cultural heterogeneity in Joyce's writings coexists with a perspective that unites 'Irish, Jewish, black, Oriental, Indian, English, Boer, palefaces, redskins, jewgreek and greekjew'[21] and breaks down the kind of binary polarization engendered by colonialism.

The exact nature of the colonial relationship between Ireland and Britain is a highly specific one, involving centuries of subjugation and settlement, but *Ulysses* was being finished as a truce was declared between British forces and the IRA and within a few weeks of the novel being finished a peace treaty between the warring sides was signed. This equivocal position, emerging out of a colonial order but not yet postcolonial, is reflected in the title for a collection of essays that appeared in 2000, *Semicolonial Joyce*, edited by Attridge and Howes. The presence of a determinate historical and cultural context in *Ulysses*, which was of fundamental importance in muddying the clear waters of postmodernist orthodoxy, is the common factor in the current work of Andrew Gibson, Len Platt and other likeminded critics. Platt's *Joyce and the Anglo-Irish* appeared in 1996 and most of its chapters are devoted to *Ulysses* and the ways in which its author reacted to the Irish Literary Revival. Andrew Gibson's *Joyce's Revenge: History, Politics, and Aesthetics in Ulysses* first published in 2002, broadens the scope and studies Joyce's novel in relation to political, social and cultural relations between Ireland and Britain in the period 1880–1920. More recently, Gibson and Platt edited a collection of essays, *Joyce, Ireland, Britain*, that brought together essays by British and Irish scholars united by a desire to relocate Joyce from the frames of international modernism or postmodernism to cultural and political relations between the colonizer and the colonized. Such an approach to *Ulysses* has produced a host of new readings of the book's episodes and shifted the cultural terrain of Joyce criticism.

The value of historically minded, materialist critics like Gibson and Platt is that they read *Ulysses* with a close attention to how Joyce wrote and an avoidance of the kind of post-colonialist theorizing that can sometimes create a barrier between the reader and text. In *Ulysses*, particularly in the 'Cyclops' episode, Joyce is seen as a writer who seeks to go well beyond the narrow confines of an Irish nationalism, which unknowingly apes the English version of an exclusive racial identity, by re-inventing what it means to be Irish. He sought to avoid the easy sentimentalizing of past failures on the part of the Irish to assert their identity, something that emerges clearly in the 'Sirens' chapter in relation to songs, without dismissing the valour of such attempts. Joyce's project is to accept the symbol of Irish art, the 'cracked lookingglass of a servant' (1.146), by acknowledging its fractured nature and creating the conditions for a new vision of citizenship that transcends mere nationality. Instead of regarding Joyce's play with styles as an exercise in modernist aesthetics, new readings of *Ulysses* explore the styles as the results of an engaged encounter with those forces, imperial and spiritual, that rule his country. Joyce takes a particular English or Anglo-Irish discourse and subjects it to a process of distortion, destroying the nature of its claim to authority so that in 'The Oxen of the Sun' chapter, for example, the idea of a sterling tradition of English prose is rendered ridiculous: 'He did to the invader what, for centuries, the invader had done to Ireland: he denied his autonomy and contaminated his purity.'[22] When Shane Leslie reviewed *Ulysses* for the *Quarterly Review* in October 1922 he described the novel as 'an attempted Clerkenwell explosion in the well-guarded, well-built, classical prison of English Literature.'[23] Leslie almost certainly did not know that the bombing of Clerkenwell prison was referred to in 'Proteus' (see page 31) though he would be even more surprised to learn that his comment would be endorsed in a positive spirit by a later generation of literary critics.

GENETIC CRITICISM

Genetic criticism of Joyce, which does not focus on one particular version of the text but rather on the process by which the text came into existence, is currently a practice principally engaged with *Finnegans Wake* but it has also yielded interesting studies of *Ulysses*. A genetic critic hopes to find clues as to the author's intention by noting and examining the choices an author has made during the production of a work. Joyce's way of composition was to jot down ideas in a series of notebooks and then, when it came to the actual writing, cross out notebook material with crayons once it had been incorporated into his text. The earliest known material that found its way into *Ulysses* was from notebooks primarily serving earlier writings such as *A Portrait of the Artist as a Young Man* and the earliest known notebook devoted exclusively to *Ulysses* is dated to around 1917. This notebook is now lost but a transcription of it was made by a friend whom Joyce had asked to copy out those notes in it which had not been crossed out. In the late 1980s two scholars, having worked like sleuths to gather and interpret from the evidence of likely source material for the transcriptions, as well as other extant *Ulysses* manuscripts, reconstructed the notebook and it was published as *The Lost Notebook*.[24]

An early genetic study of *Ulysses* was A. Walton Litz's *The Art of James Joyce*, published in 1964, followed by Michael Groden's *Ulysses in Progress* in 1977. Groden studied the various notebooks, drafts and typescripts relating to the composition of *Ulysses*, which had ended up in the British Library and a number of university libraries in the United States, and showed how Joyce's style evolved over time in the writing of his novel. The ultimate work of Joyce's genetic criticism is the *Joyce Archives*, 63 volumes containing facsimiles of every surviving piece of writing by the author, with 16 volumes devoted to *Ulysses*.

The 16 volumes helped explain why there was still no definitive edition of *Ulysses* by the time the *Joyce Archives* were published in the late 1970s. Due to the existence of various sets of proofs and typescripts, there was an absence of any authoritative, original manuscript. In 1984 a team of German editors led by Hans Walter Gabler brought out a revised edition in three volumes and two years later it appeared as a one-volume Corrected Text. It was the result of seven years' work and claimed to have made five thousand alterations to established texts, though most of these were so minor as to make little difference to the reader. The new edition was subjected to severe criticism by some scholars, led by the then-unknown John Kidd, but it has established itself as the standard reference. The attacks on the editorial principles of Gabler's team, however, inflicted damage on the claim to have produced a definitive edition.

CHAPTER 5

ADAPTATION, INTERPRETATION AND INFLUENCE

LITERARY INFLUENCE

It is no exaggeration to say that *Ulysses* has changed irrevocably, the history of prose fiction. Joyce's novel quickly established itself as a canonical work of literature that broke new ground in ways of writing and it influenced many authors in the 1920s and 1930s. Some of Joyce's techniques were particularly influential in the work of Virginia Woolf, despite the infamous criticism of *Ulysses* in her diary as an 'underbred' work by a 'self-taught working man'. In an unpublished notebook she records reading it with 'spasms of wonder, of discovery'[1] and the effect of some of this wonder can be seen in *Mrs Dalloway* (1925). Woolf's novel echoes the 'Wandering Rocks' chapter in the way characters occupy the same urban space as they go about their quotidian business, with the use of multiple perspectives and interior monologue common to both novels. The stream of consciousness technique, particularly Joyce's way of catching thoughts before they are grammatically articulated, is used by Woolf in poetic ways of her own. As in *Ulysses*, the sections of *Mrs Dalloway* are divided by simple breaks in the text and the book as a whole is structured around the course of one day; both authors paid careful attention to the passing hours and plotted their stories accordingly.

Major modern writers like Jorge Luis Borges, Vladimir Nabokov, Umberto Eco and Salman Rushdie have all testified to the positive influence of reading *Ulysses*, bearing witness to F. Scott Fitzgerald's prediction in 1923 that Joyce would be 'the most profound literary influence in the next fifty years'.[2] In this respect, too, the works of

Raymond Queneau, Italo Calvino, Philip Roth, Georges Perec and Thomas Pynchon have all been evoked. Rushdie's *The Satanic Verses* is an exemplar of certain aspects of Joyce's literary influence: its intertextuality and free-wheeling polystylism and what Krishna Sen has called 'the chutnification of the colonizer's language'[3]. Joyce's potent influence on Indian writers has been traced in G.V. Desani's *All About H. Hatte* (1948) and in his introduction to Desani's novel Anthony Burgess relates it to *Ulysses* in its structure and its 'gloriously impure' approach to the English language.[4]

The first translation of the whole of *Ulysses* was into German in 1927 (a French translation came out two years later) and, to avoid possible prosecution, it appeared without mentioning the publisher's name. It had a powerful effect on contemporary German writers and its influence on Alfred Döblin was immediate. Döblin was writing *Berlin Alexanderplatz* at the time and in 1928, a year before his novel was published, he reviewed *Ulysses* and praised it as a new class of city novel: 'To the experiential image of a person today also belongs the streets, the scenes changing by the seconds, the signboards, automobile traffic.'[5] There is little doubt that his reading of *Ulysses* influenced the way multiple perspectives operate in *Berlin Alexanderplatz* and the way in which the novel uses newspapers, sound effects and speeches. Two other important German novels published after the German translation of *Ulysses*, Hans Henny Jahnn's *Perrudja* (1929) and Hermann Broch's *The Sleepwalkers* (1931), also show the influence of Joyce's work.[6] Later German writers, even if they did not read the German-language edition of *Ulysses*, would have been introduced to Joyce's style of writing through their acquaintance with *Berlin Alexanderplatz* and *Perrudja*.

Anthony Burgess himself was a devoted Joycean and wrote five books about his favourite author: *Joysprick*, bringing a linguistic approach to Joyce's writing, two introductions to the author, *Rejoyce* and *Here Comes Everybody*, a shortened version of *Finnegans Wake*, and the less well known libretto to a musical interpretation of *Ulysses* entitled *Blooms of Dublin* that was produced in 1982. As a young man Joyce had considered making a career out of his accomplished singing and Burgess shared his twin interests in writing and music. There are similarities in the artistic temperaments of Joyce and Burgess – their deep sense of the comic and a relish for puns and word play reflecting a near obsession with the workings of language – but it is hard to say to what extent Joyce influenced

Burgess and to what extent the English writer found in Joyce a humour allied to his own.

For some Irish writers, the issue was not one of responding in kind to a kindred spirit but something quite contrary; Joyce looming almost forbiddingly over their work, as if daring them to emulate or rival what he achieved. The figure who bears the most eloquent testimony to this is Samuel Beckett. The young Beckett became Joyce's friend in Paris and generously helped him in his work, working as a kind of unpaid secretary out of devotion to the man. Joyce appreciated this and in 1938, when Beckett was attacked and stabbed by a pimp, Joyce got to his bedside as quickly as possible and besides paying for him to have a private room in the hospital lent him his favourite reading lamp. 'When I came to,' recalled Beckett, the first thing I remember was Joyce standing at the end of the ward and coming to see me.'[7] The younger writer struggled to find his own voice, noting how his early writing 'stinks of Joyce in spite of most earnest endeavours to endow it with my own odours' and vowed 'I will get over JJ ere I die. Yessir.'[8] They met for the last time in a village they both passed through when fleeing the Nazis after the German occupation of Paris in 1940.

Seamus Heaney's engagement with Joyce, as a fellow writer and fellow Irishman, is also of notable interest. In the twelfth verse of 'Station Island' (1984), Joyce is the unnamed mentor whose steadying presence comes before the poet-speaker: 'wintered hard and sharp as a blackthorn bush. / His voice eddying with the vowels of all rivers'.[9] Joyce urges him to strike out on his own, reject the lure of self-abnegation and write only for the joy it will bring him. Years earlier, in 'Traditions' (1972), Bloom's riposte to the Citizen about his Irishness (12.1431) is cited by Heaney to assert in linguistic terms his pluralist and proud sense of identity.[10] In *The Redress of Poetry* (1995), Heaney returns to *Ulysses* and Joyce's attempt 'to marginalise the imperium which had marginalised him by replacing the Anglocentric Protestant tradition with a newly forged apparatus of Homeric correspondences, Dantesque scholasticism and a more or less Mediterranean, European, classically endorsed world-view'.[11]

Other Irish poets have acknowledged the impact of reading *Ulysses*, whether in their own poetry or in prose statements. Thomas Kinsella's 1997 collection of poems, *The Pen Shop*, bears conscious echoes of Bloom's journey across Dublin while Paul Muldoon remembers the effect of reading in the opening 'Telemachus' chapter of the milkwoman pouring milk into Stephen's measure (1.397–407). The milkwoman becomes a messenger representing a traditional, folksy Ireland (see page 25): 'To serve or to upbraid, whether he could not tell: but scorned to beg her favour.' It registered as a 'luminous moment' for Muldoon:

> The fact that Joyce did not beg any favours from that image of Ireland . . . was enormously liberating to me . . . His act of resistance took place in time. But the passage of time has only made clearer that it was not a temporal act. The fact that he was defiant, and anti-iconic, and that as a young man he faced the dream and enticement of a particular image of Ireland with so much courage and refusal has been for me, as for so many others, a saving grace.[12]

ULYSSES IN MUSIC AND FILM

Joyce's interest in music was not something incidental to his work – after all, there are more than 700 musical allusions in *Ulysses* – and Burgess was not alone in composing music as a way of paying homage to the writer. One of the first significant electronic works of the Italian composer Luciano Berio (1925–2003) was *Thema (Omaggio a Joyce)*, based on the fugue-like opening of the 'Sirens' chapter (see page 58). In 1958, Berio taped his wife reading the lines before electronically modifying the recording, producing a hybrid work that seeks to explore the overlapping contours of speech and music. Less avant-garde introductions to the musical dimension in *Ulysses* are available to the reader by way of recordings of some of the popular songs, ballads, music hall numbers and operatic airs that weave their way in and around the text of *Ulysses* (see page 118). Another original musical homage to Joyce's novel comes from the rock group Jefferson Airplane with the song 'Rejoyce', on their famed 1967 album *After Bathing at Baxters*. Kate Bush was also inspired by Joyce's text to write some original music but, being refused permission by the Joyce Estate to release it, re-wrote the lyrics to keep the rhythm and feeling of the words but without breaching copyright. 'The song was saying "Yes, Yes" and when I asked for permission they said "No! No!", she explained in 1989.

The songs and music referred to in *Ulysses* can be reproduced through modern recordings as well as lending themselves to cinematic renditions but conveying the novel's textual depth through film would present a supreme challenge to anyone and, perhaps wisely, has not been attempted – although it is tempting to hypothesize about what might have been the result had Eisenstein (1898–1948) made a film of *Ulysses*. The filmmaker and Joyce met once in Paris in 1929 and it is said they discussed the possibility of turning the book into a film. Eisenstein certainly read *Ulysses* and he was interested in the idea of filming a character's thoughts; in a 1934 lecture at the Russian State Institute of Cinematography he drew attention to the importance of Joyce's use of interior monologue for the cinema. Perhaps they even influenced one another for the possibility has been proposed that the 'Wandering Rocks' chapter was influenced by Eisenstein's concept of montage. What is known is that Joyce enjoyed the cinema and despite problems with his eyesight watched films on many occasions. In the 1930s, it seems, he was contacted by Warner Brothers about movie rights for *Ulysses* but Joyce rejected the idea on the grounds of 'artistic propriety'.[13] Back in 1909, on one of his rare return visits to Dublin, an entrepreneurial Joyce had been intent on setting up the city's first cinema; a commercial enterprise backed by capital from a group of Triestine businessmen. He found suitable premises in the centre of the city and in December of that year produced a cinematographic show there for the public. The plan was eventually to establish cinemas in a number of Irish cities but the businessmen in Trieste backed out and the whole enterprise collapsed.

The degree of success achieved by the two film versions of *Ulysses* that have been made is largely confined to their management of the novel's plot. The first, by the American director Joseph Strick in 1967, was banned in Ireland (and not released there for public viewing until 2000, the longest film ban in Irish film history) and was subjected in New Zealand to screenings that segregated male and female viewers. This makes Strick's film seem far more erotic and explicit than it actually is but the use of the word 'fuck', one of the first times the word was heard in a film, created consternation in the minds of censors. The setting is blatantly 1960s Dublin – little attempt was made at recreating the novel's period – but the city has changed so much in half a century as to give the film a dated charm and historicity. For viewers today, the resulting semblance of a bygone age functions as a substitute for the actual turn-of-the-century setting that Joyce intended. To his credit, Strick does not take liberties with the novel's text and the film bravely takes on the phantasmological nature of the 'Circe' episode. In a way, too, the 'Penelope' episode succeeds in places in capturing the chapter's mood of resigned acceptance and the lone female voice in a very masculine world.

A more recent film version was released in 2003, entitled *Bloom* and directed by Sean Walsh. The casting for Molly Bloom would not strike everyone as successful and Stephen Rhea as Leopold, unlike Milo O'Shea in Strick's film, comes across as too doleful, lacking the essential sanguinity that is so endearingly an aspect of the character he plays. Passages of interior monologue are rendered by straightforward voiceovers and the overall effect is a static one, though the same could not be said for the lively 'Penelope' episode which opens the film as well as ending it. As with Strick's version, *Bloom* does have the virtue of not radically departing from Joyce's text and both films offer a way into the novel's narrative for the new reader.

There are two other short films, both made for British television, that serve to introduce the novel: *James Joyce's Ulysses* was made in 1988 as part of the Modern World: Ten Great Writers series and mixed a documentary-style presentation with selected dramatizations starring David Suchet as Leopold Bloom and Sorcha Cusask as Molly; and *Ulysses*, broadcast in 2001 by the BBC, was a documentary narrated by Tom Paulin.

A short documentary film, *The Bloom Mystery*, directed by Csilla Toldy (www.csillatoldy.com) focuses on the Hungarian–Jewish origins of Leopold Bloom. The film was shot on Bloomsday 2007, in Hungary and Ireland, and bears original testimony to the international appeal of Joyce's novel. *Joyce to the World*, directed by Fritzi Horstman, is a 58-minute documentary (2004) about *Ulysses*, featuring actors, writers and scholars in a celebration of Bloomsday. *A Shout from the Streets*, a 26-minute film inspired by *Ulysses* and made by Fred DeVecca in 2000, takes its title from the conversation between Stephen Dedalus and Mr Deasy in the 'Nestor' chapter (2.380–6).

ULYSSES IN ART

Joyce's friend Frank Budgen, author of *James Joyce and the Making of Ulysses*, was the first artist to attempt illustrating *Ulysses* and he was shortly followed by Henri Matisse who was commissioned to illustrate a de luxe edition of the novel published in New York in 1935 by the Limited Editions Club. Budgen, unlike Matisse, was very familiar with the novel and this is reflected in his work. His illustration for the 'Nausicaa' episode, for example, shows fireworks and a bat in the evening sky, both mentioned in the text, while the shadowy scene is tellingly contrasted with the white underskirt of Gerty's and the figure of Bloom looking on with one hand in his pocket. Matisse, by comparison, worked from an acquaintance with Homer's *Odyssey* and his etchings support the common assumption that he never read Joyce's novel. The Australian artist Sidney Nolan (1917–92) did read *Ulysses* and produced a series of works as a direct result (unfortunately, only one survives) and so did the Italian artist Mimmo Paladino (b.1948) who was commissioned by the Folio Society to illustrate their 1998 edition of the novel. The Franklin Library in Pennsylvania brought out three illustrated editions in the 1970s and used a different artist (Alan E. Cober, Paul Hogarth and Kenneth Francis Dewey) each time. In 1988 there was another limited edition of the novel, this time illustrated by the American abstract expressionist painter Robert Motherwell (1915–91) in etchings and aquatints.

British artist Richard Hamilton, born three weeks after the first publication of *Ulysses* in 1922, first read Joyce's novel as a young man doing National Service in 1947. The reading experience inaugurated a life-long engagement with the book and a life-long influence on his work as an artist. Joyce's play with style, his instinct for pastiche, rejection of tradition and embrace of low and high culture, even his meticulous work methods, are all characteristics that Hamilton has referenced as influences on his own artistic development. Given Hamilton's own influence on Warhol and Pop Art this suggests the possibility of an impressive Joycean heritage in the world of art.

Hamilton's reading of the book inspired him to work on a set of preliminary drawings with the idea of creating a new illustrated edition of *Ulysses*. The plan was to produce eighteen different illustrations, one for each chapter of the book, not primarily seeking a pictorial representation by way of depicting specific event but working instead on a different style for each picture. Although some drawings were publicly shown in 1950, as part of a Joyce exhibition at the Institute of Contemporary Arts in London, the larger scheme was stymied by production difficulties and, as a director with the publisher Faber pointed out (T. S. Eliot), the costs of such an ambitious project. In 1981, prompted by the forthcoming centenary of Joyce's birth, Hamilton planned a series of intaglio prints. The first of these which he executed, entitled 'In Horne's house' after the name of the chief doctor at the hospital in the 'Oxen of the Sun' chapter, gives a clear idea of how his thinking and artistry had evolved.

In 1949, Hamilton had made a pen and ink study with watercolour of the 'Oxen of the Sun' episode but he was dissatisfied with the way its Cubist vocabulary fell short of reflecting the parody of the English prose tradition that characterized the form of Joyce's chapter. In the 1980s he re-worked an earlier study: 'I completely revamped it to include the concept of a developing flow of styles from earliest to modern.'[14] In its final version Hamilton parallels Joyce's embryological movement of language with nine stages from art history, beginning with an archaic Easter Island- style head and 'progressing' through ancient Egyptian art, the Italian Renaissance with the nurse as a Bellini Madonna, Rembrandt, a stirring Stephen Dedalus in the style of Napoleon by the French Romantic Baron Gros, Bloom as a Cézanne bourgeois, the tin of sardines rendered in a Cubist still life, Futurist drinking glasses and a 'non-objective abstraction which serves as the composition's stable focal point'.[15]

A similar kind of confluence between Hamilton's art and Joyce's writing reveals itself in his etching 'Bronze by gold', depicting the barmaids from the 'Sirens' chapter, the bronze-haired Miss Douce and the golden-haired Miss Kennedy, with Joyce's intertextuality finding a parallel in the visual echoes of Manet's 'A Bar at the Folies-Bergère' and the School of Fontainebleau's 'Gabrielle d'Estrées and One of Her Sisters' in Hamilton's work. In 1998, the artist turned to digital technology to produce 'The heaventree of stars', an arresting work derived from the line in 'Ithaca' describing the night sky: 'The heaventree of stars hung with humid nightblue fruit' (17.1039).

One of Hamilton's works, 'Finn MacCool', is somewhat question-able in terms of its fidelity to Joyce. The citizen in the 'Cyclops' chapter is a brutal bigot but it was a photograph of Raymond Pius McCartney, an IRA hunger-striker in the Maze prison in Northern Ireland, that stimulated Hamilton to re-work his earlier depiction of Joyce's Cyclops as a Celtic giant and present him in his 1983 work as a hirsute, blanketed prisoner. The suggestion that the narrow-minded and virulently anti-semitic citizen of 'Cyclops' might best be repre-sented by a political prisoner in the Maze prison is a contentious one and the confusion this may give rise to is reflected in a Hamilton oil painting exhibited in London's Tate Gallery. This painting, enti-tled 'The citizen' and also depicting an IRA hunger-striker, depicts a Christ-like figure gazing serenely at the viewer with swirls of his own excreta forming the background. It is a powerful portrayal of human dignity but seems to have little in common with the belligerent bully found in Barney Kiernan's pub.

A number of other modern artists have produced work that responds to *Ulysses* at different levels and much of their work was brought together at a Joyce in Art exhibition at the RHA Gallery in Dublin in 2004 to coincide with the ReJoyce Dublin celebrations that marked the centenary of 16 June 1904. The exhibition included excerpts from the work of Joseph Beuys (1921–86) who, beginning in the late 1950s, worked for a number of years on a set of drawings that he declared were an extension of *Ulysses*. The exhibition also paid homage to a piece of *Ulysses*-inspired art by the Irish installation and video artist James Colman (b.1941) who in 1982, the centenary of Joyce's birth, decorated the bricked-up door of 7 Eccles Street with a garland of xeranthemum leaves, one kind of the plants called 'everlasting'. A silver cast of the garland was on show at the Joyce in Art exhibition while the door itself, when the house was demolished, became a piece of installation art in its own right when it ended up on exhibition at the James Joyce Centre in Dublin.

CANNIBALIZING *ULYSSES*

Cannibal Joyce is the title of a book about the way Joyce's writing creatively expropriates literary traditions and various cultural forms but the trope also serves as a way of describing the manner in which the book has become a commodity – and possibly a fetish to some – and the way different aspects of it are taken and incorporated in something else.[16] Such is the novel's daunting density of allusions that its totalizing, encyclopaedic nature and its complexity of form constitute an inexhaustible source of material for literary critics of virtually any persuasion. By the same token, the afterlife of *Ulysses* continues to thrive because the novel has a healthy resistance to any and all theoretical paradigms that would dare to contain it: humanism, realism, neo-Marxism, linguistics, psychoanalysis, feminism, structuralism, post-structuralism, modernism, postmodernism, cultural studies, post-colonialism, genetic studies. All of these approaches have been and are being applied to Joyce's novel and they often yield interesting and insightful re-readings but in the process an industry has been created, slag has been deposited and a Joyce discourse institutionalized. Academic careers, from postgraduate dissertations to tenured posts, have progressed with the writing of yet more books and articles about *Ulysses*; as far back as 1951, a time that now seems virginal in terms of Joyce-inspired enterprises, Patrick Kavanagh was provoked into writing his poem 'Who Killed James Joyce?'

> What weapon was used
> To slay mighty Ulysses?
> The weapon that was used
> Was a Harvard thesis.[17]

Such a sentiment cannot be applied to what occurred in 1967 when Thomas F. Stanley at the University of Tulsa, then editor of the recently created *James Joyce Quarterly*, along with Fritz Senn in Zurich and Bernard Benstock, then at Kent State University, organized the first International James Joyce Symposium in Dublin. The James Joyce Foundation was established at this Symposium with the laudable aim of encouraging scholarship and the exchange of ideas between readers. In 1988 it became the International James Joyce Foundation and it now sponsors the International Symposia that take place every two years in a different European city. In the years between, a North America Joyce Conference takes place. There was a break after the seventh symposium in 1979, to allow for the eighth one to coincide with the centenary of Joyce's birth, and the 1982 symposium in Dublin attracted over 500 registrants. The President of Ireland was in attendance and he officiated at the dedication of a bust of Joyce in St. Stephen's Green. Hugh Kenner was given the honour of unveiling a plaque on the house at 52 Upper Clanbrassil St where Leopold Bloom was born while the Taoiseach Charles Haughey hosted an official reception at Dublin Castle. Along with Anthony Burgess and Simon and Garfunkel, one of the guests was Tom Stoppard whose play *Travesties* (1975) had toyed with the possibility that when Joyce was in Zurich in 1917 writing *Ulysses* he could have encountered Lenin and the Dadaist poet Tristan Tzara, two other residents of the city at that time. By 1990, the Symposium reached its nadir when it was held in glitzy Monaco and proved too expensive an event for many who might have wished to attend.

The year 1982 also signalled the arrival of 16 June as an event that would become increasingly important in Ireland's tourist calendar. What would become known as Bloomsday was first celebrated in 1954 when a small number of enthusiasts organized what turned into a daylong *Ulysses* pilgrimage. At that time Joyce was not approved of in Ireland and the Minister for External Affairs had refused to open a James Joyce exhibition in Paris. Irish academics also ignored Joyce and it was a handful of the country's writers – Flann O'Brien and Patrick Kavanagh being the best known ones – who organized the homage to *Ulysses* on the fiftieth anniversary of its events. They met outside the Martello tower in Sandycove and set off in two horse-drawn cabs to retrace the route of the funeral procession and visit a number of pubs along the way. For Bloomsday in 1982 there was a recreation of the 'Wandering Rocks' episode by around one hundred participants in period costume, riding in horse-drawn coaches along the route of the novel's viceregal procession through Dublin.

Bloomsday is now a well-established event, marketed with gusto by the authorities, usually kicking off with merrymaking in period costume at the Martello tower and at lunchtime invariably featuring Davy Byrne's pub serving Burgundy and gorgonzola (as enjoyed there by Bloom). Various dramatisations, walking tours, readings and lectures complete the scene. Bloomsday 2004 marked the centenary of the novel's events and was a tourist-oriented extravaganza in Dublin supported by the country's Establishment in a way that could only charitably be called ironic, given the way Ireland treated Joyce in his lifetime (it was left to Bruce Arnold, one of the speakers at the International James Joyce Symposium that also took place in Dublin that year, to use the word hypocrisy). The National Library of Ireland opened its *James Joyce and Ulysses* exhibition with touch screens for visitors to digitally turn the pages of four of the *Ulysses* notebooks held by the library. Joyce and *Ulysses* are now big business: Irish postage stamps and bank notes have been issued bearing his image, the first one hundred copies of the first edition, signed by the author, are valued at over £100,000 each and richly endowed libraries in the US, but also the National Library of Ireland, have paid colossal sums for copies of manuscripts, letters and note books written by Joyce. As part of the 2004 anniversary even Google altered its trademark logo for the day to weave in Joyce and some of his fictional characters, and celebratory events and high jinks took place across the world. Even in the small town of Szombathely in Hungary – the fictional birthplace of Bloom's father – Bloomsday has been celebrated since 1994 (see page 104).

What is remarkable about the legacy of *Ulysses* is the way in which it has impacted on high and low culture, non-professional enthusiasts and university teachers, commercially minded sponsors and publicly funded institutions. There seems to be no limits to the catholicity of its appeal (though this is probably inversely proportional to the number of people who have actually read the book). On the one hand there are plaques pasted to the walls of thoroughly modernized premises in Ireland announcing its James Joyce Pub Award as an 'authentic Irish pub'. The plaques change the line in *Ulysses* 'Good puzzle would be cross Dublin without passing a pub' (4.129–30) to read 'cross Ireland without passing a pub', presumably to allow for the marketing of the award to pubs outside of Dublin. At the other extreme there are renowned scholars like Fritz Senn who have managed to bridge the gap between academia and amateurism. Baulking at remarks like 'I teach Joyce' and issuing 'Ten Simple Rules' for producing maximum boredom at Joyce conferences, Senn bears personal testimony to the value of a Joyce community rather than a Joyce industry.[18]

LACAN AND *ULYSSES*

Lacan was in his seventies when he addressed an International Joyce Symposium in Paris in 1975 and recalled having seen Joyce in a Paris bookshop in 1921. In his address he spoke of Joyce as 'The Sinthome' (an old spelling of *symptôme*) and this became the title of Lacan's twenty-third seminar (1975–6). The influence of Joyce on Lacan's theoretical elaborations is not clear-cut and much of what Lacan says is based on his idea of the significance of *Finnegans Wake* rather than *Ulysses*; and with both texts it is debateable how much was actually read by Lacan. At a broad psychoanalytic level, Joyce is seen as struggling with an absent, inadequate father and the son's constant writing is an attempt to supplement this fundamental lack and avoid psychosis. Joyce cannot help but echo his father's symptoms – exemplified by an excessive drinking at the expense of his family – while battling to protect his daughter Lucia against the onset of a mental deterioration that led to her being institutionalized in 1934. Issues of paternity wave their way through *Ulysses* but Lacan does not engage in any close readings and his remarks remain general ones.

The nature of Joyce's influence on Lacan remains a subject for debate. Not all of Lacan's writings are available in English, including 'The Sinthome', and critics equally at home with Joyce's fiction and

Lacanian psychoanalysis are rare. What seems clear is that through Joyce Lacan crystallized his new understanding of the term 'symptom', no longer regarding it as just a coded message from the unconscious but seeing it now as a mode of being for the *jouissance* of the subject. Joyce's writing stands for, embodies, a *sinthome* – a signifying formation centred around a kernel of pure enjoyment, a binding quantum. It overwhelms the symbolic order that underlies conventional fiction. Joyce identified with his symptom, as a way of organizing and making possible his life, and by the creation of his ego he lived with himself. Joyce as a *sinthome* knots together and reconstitutes the uneasy partnership of the Real, Symbolic and Imaginary. A *sinthome* is also life-fulfilling; it channels out a consistency of being which is adhered to with, in Joyce's case at least, a complete fidelity.

CHAPTER 6

GUIDE TO FURTHER READING

Books' full publication details, unless given below, are to be found in the bibliography.

EDITIONS OF *ULYSSES*

There are various editions of *Ulysses* and for the new reader the choice is complicated by the way copyright issues continue to bedevil the form adopted by different publishers. The now standard edition, the so-called Corrected Text published in 1986 and edited by Hans Walter Gabler, comes with little or no critical apparatus other than chapter numbers printed at the bottom of each page and lines numbered separately for each chapter. Given that many British and American editions, both hardback and paperback, use the same page and line numbers plus the fact that nearly all post-1986 references to *Ulysses* use this text, it has become fairly indispensable for readers. It is the one used in this book.

Ulysses: Annotated Student Edition (1992), published by Penguin, has an introduction and a useful set of notes by Declan Kiberd but the line-numbering system begins anew on each page and is only useful in conjunction with the notes at the back of the book. The eighteen chapters are not numbered on the page and this makes it difficult to quickly locate a particular episode.

Johnson, Jeri. ed. (2008), *Ulysses: The 1922 text*. Oxford: Oxford University Press. This Oxford World Classics edition has a very useful critical apparatus which includes an introduction, a short history of the novel's composition and publication, notes at the back for each chapter and reproductions of the Gilbert and Linati schemas. Unfortunately, it does not have a line- or chapter-numbering system.

Works of criticism on *Ulysses* published before the Corrected Text refer to various older editions of the book, principally the 1961 Random House one, and this can prove time-consuming when trying to trace particular references. Cross-references to the various editions, arranged in chronological order starting with the 1922 Shakespeare and Company edition, are provided in Gunn, Ian and McCleery, Alistair. (1988), *The Ulysses Pagefinder*. Edinburgh: Split Pea Press.

Danis Rose. ed. (2004), *Ulysses The Reader's Edition*. Mousehole, Cornwall: Houyhnhnm Press. This edition has had a troubled history and a new edition was published in 2004 to comply with a court ruling that had outlawed Rose's original 1997 edition. Although the 2004 version has removed the notorious punctuation that Rose introduced to the 'Penelope' chapter in the 1997 edition, other eccentric editorial decisions remain.

HOMERIC LINKS

There are two first-rate, modern translations of Homer's *Odyssey*: Lattimore, Richard. (1967), *The Odyssey of Homer*. New York: Harper & Row; and Fagles, Robert. (1996), *Homer The Odyssey*. London: Penguin.

Neither of these editions was around when twelve-year-old Joyce was first introduced to the adventures of Odysseus at Clongowes College. What he read at school was Charles Lamb's *The Adventures of Ulysses*, first published in 1808, and it was this edition that he recommended to his aunt Josephine when she expressed puzzlement with *Ulysses* after its publication in 1922. Lamb's book remains an accessible introduction to Homer's epic and is available in a modern edition: Lamb, Charles. (1992), *The Adventures of Ulysses*, ed. John Cooke. Edinburgh: Split Pea Press.

Stuart Gilbert's study was first published in 1930 and still offers an illuminating account of Homeric correspondences in the novel. For readers interested in pursuing the Homeric dimension to *Ulysses*, there is a relevant chapter in Schork, R. J. (1998), *Greek and Hellenic Culture in Joyce*. Gainesville, FL: University Press of Florida. For a more general cultural history of Homer's *Odyssey* and its continuing presence in modern culture there is Hall, Edith. (2008), *The Return of Ulysses*. London: I. B. Tauris.

BIOGRAPHIES

Richard Ellmann's magisterial but problematic biography, revised in 1982, remains the standard reference when it comes to biographical information but for shorter and insightful introductions to the life, times and writings of Joyce there are Ian Pindar's *Joyce* (2004), and Andrew Gibson's *James Joyce* (2006). It was in Trieste that significant sections of *Ulysses* were written and this period of Joyce's life is covered with fresh insights in McCourt, John. (2001), *The Years of Bloom: James Joyce in Trieste, 1904–1920*. Dublin: Lilliput Press.

ANNOTATED GUIDES

Joyce's compilatory skills are so astonishing, the level of his erudition so deep and the range of his reach into Dublin life and culture so wide that assistance is required for 'Sherlockholmesing' *Ulysses (16.831)*. Given the encyclopaedic range of references and the obliquity with which Joyce's knowledge is poured into the novel, it is often difficult to even know that an allusion is there to be appreciated. Readers with some knowledge of Irish history, for example, will have come across the gist of Robert Emmet's speech from the dock after being sentenced to death and they will know that this is being referred to as the 'Sirens' chapter draws to a close but it requires a helpful nudge to appreciate that, after saying 'When my country takes her place among the nations of the earth, then, and not till then, let my epitaph be written', Emmet concluded with the words 'I have done.' Without this knowledge the full force of the chapter's conclusion and its play on the word 'done' is not available to the reader. An understanding of parts of *Ulysses* is especially dependent on a knowledge of the references and an annotated list becomes invaluable. In 'Scylla and Charybdis' there are so many allusions to Shakespeare, not just his plays but details of his life, that the reader needs help in order to appreciate the knowledge (and often the irony) that Stephen Dedalus is putting to work in support of his thesis.

There are two books offering annotated notes for *Ulysses* and the best is Gifford, Don and Seidman, Robert J. (2008), *Ulysses Annotated*. Berkeley, CA: University of California Press. This is an impressive work of scholarship, helpfully keyed to both Gabler's Corrected Text and the 1961 Random House editions, and is fairly essential for readers seeking explication of details in Joyce's novel.

The other book of annotations is Thornton, Weldon. (1968), *Allusions in Ulysses: An Annotated List*. Chapel Hill, NC: University of North Carolina Press. The book follows the chapters of *Ulysses* and each reference to the text is given by page and line numbers to the 1961 and 1934 Random House (or Modern Library) editions. This is fine if using one of those but many readers will have a copy of the novel based on Hans Walter Gabler's edition of 1984 and the page and line numbers will not correspond.

READING AND WALKING GUIDES

Blamires, Harry. (1996), *The New Bloomsday Book*. London: Routledge. This guide has helped many first-time readers because of its detailed page-by-page summaries. The third edition, published in 1996, is keyed into the Gabler Corrected Text, Penguin and Oxford World Classics editions.

An especially useful reading guide is *Ulysses Unbound* by Terrence Killeen (2005). Each episode in the novel is summarized in some detail, followed by a theory-free account of its style and a more general commentary of issues raised by the episode. Further episode-based sections cover the principal people and events, followed by a glossary of foreign language words and phrases.

Nicholson, Robert. (2002), *The Ulysses Guide*. Dublin: New Island. No visit to Dublin is complete without a copy of Nicholson's guide. It offers a series of eight walking tours, each with their own map, grouped around those parts of various chapters that share common ground. The walks are written with the new reader in mind and the links between places and plot are explained with admirable clarity.

Robert Nicholson, the curator of the James Joyce Tower & Museum at Sandycove (the tower which features in the novel's opening chapter), is also the presenter of *James Joyce's Dublin: The Ulysses Tour*, a DVD released by Artsmagic in 2007. Its chapter-by-chapter structure uses the relevant street locations in and around Dublin and the instructive commentary provides an accurate and useful introduction to the plot of *Ulysses* as well as offering readers visual markers for many of the key scenes in the novel.

Compiled by Katherine McSharry. (2004), *A Joycean Scrapbook*. Bray: Wordwell in association with the National Library of Ireland. This collection of Joyce-related pictorial material relating to the popular culture of early twentieth-century Dublin, plus a section on Joyce's life abroad, can be recommended to readers of *Ulysses*.

More pictorial material relating to *Ulysses* is to be found in Niall Murphy. (2004), *A Bloomsday Postcard*. Dublin: Lilliput Press (in association with the National Library of Ireland). The author has assembled 250 postcards, all of them posted in the Dublin area during 1904, that illustrate various moments in the text. The post-cards are grouped under the novel's chapters and are accompanied by chapter summaries.

LITERARY CRITICISM

The American writer Max Eastman asked Joyce why he wrote in such a difficult style and the author is said to have replied that he wanted to keep scholars busy for 300 years. His wish seems likely to be fulfilled and there is already a colossal amount of literary criti-cism confronting students of *Ulysses*; the books below are merely the tip of an iceberg that threatens to bewilder, if not sink, the unwary reader.

Hugh Kenner's *Joyce's Voices* (1978) and Colin MacCabe's *James Joyce and the Revolution of the Word* (1979) are two landmarks in Joyce criticism, written around the same time and on the same sub-ject, which could hardly be more unlike each other; both are worth consulting. Two very readable accounts that share a historical per-spective are Len Platt's *Joyce and the Anglo-Irish: A Study of Joyce and the Literary Revival* (1998) and Andrew Gibson's *Joyce's Revenge* (2005). Gibson's book, subtitled 'History, Politics, and Aesthetics in *Ulysses*', was first published in 2002 and is highly recommended. The Attridge and Howes (2000) collection brings together essays by noted critics who share a post-colonialist perspective on Joyce but for an excellent introduction to this way of reading Joyce see the 'James Joyce and Mythic Realism' chapter in Kiberd, Declan. (1996), *Invent-ing Ireland*. London: Vintage.

Andrew Gibson and Len Platt are the editors of a valuable collec-tion of essays, *Joyce, Ireland, Britain* (2006) that arose from the London University Seminar for Research into *Ulysses* at Royal Hol-loway, University of London. The essays explore historical readings of Joyce's work and taken as a whole they represent some of the best of recent Joyce criticism. Katherine Mullin's essay, 'English Vice and Irish Vigilance: the Nationality of Obscenity in *Ulysses*', Clare Hutton's

'Joyce, the Library Episode, and the Institutions of Revivalism' and John Nash's 'Irish Audiences and English Readers: The Cultural Politics of Shane Leslie's *Ulysses* Reviews' are recommended.

Pierce, David. (2008), *Reading Joyce*. Harlow: Pearson Longman. The author has been teaching Joyce for a number of years and this reader-friendly book, a distillation of his experience in many ways, includes seminar handouts, classroom experience and students' responses to Joyce. It is aimed at first-time readers of Joyce and there are three chapters devoted to *Ulysses* plus a generous spread of informative photographs throughout the book.

Brown, Richard. ed. (2008), *A Companion to James Joyce*. Oxford: Blackwell, the third of its kind entitled 'a companion' to Joyce, has essays by Maud Ellmann, John McCourt and Declan Kiberd that are especially relevant to *Ulysses* and well worth reading. A more theory-led set of essays makes up Milesi Laurent. ed. (2003), *James Joyce and the Difference of Language*. Cambridge: Cambridge University Press. One of these, 'Border Disputes' by Ellen Carol Jones, illumines the 'Oxen of the Sun' chapter with the help of Homi Bhabha's concept of hybridity, while Fritz Senn's 'Syntactic glides', written in a refreshing jargon-free way, conducts micro analyses of some textual moments in *Ulysses* to reveal how Joyce plays with troubled syntax and grammar.

Recent work includes McCourt, John. ed. (2009), *James Joyce in Context*. Cambridge: Cambridge University Press. There are over 30 essays in this collection, divided into three sections, and the first section covering biographical and publishing history has an incisive piece by Finn Fordham on why a new Joyce biography is necessary and why it probably will not be written for some time to come. The second section is devoted to critical responses and includes useful overviews of post-structuralism, gender studies, psychoanalysis, post-colonialism and genetic criticism in relation to Joyce studies. The book's third section covers cultural and historical contexts, not just familiar ones like the Irish Revival and music but also medicine, philosophy, science, religion and sex.

What is seen as overlapping areas of concern between Lacanian psychoanalysis and Joyce are explored in Brivic, Shelly. (2009), *Joyce Through Lacan and Zizek*. Basingstoke: Palgrave. Three chapters are devoted to *Ulysses* but it helps to have some acquaintance with Lacan and the best introduction to this field is Homer, Sean. (2005), *Jacques Lacan*. Routledge: London.

ADAPTATION, INTERPRETATION AND INFLUENCE

Richard Hamilton's *Imaging James Joyce's Ulysses* brings together all the prints and studies that the artist produced between 1948 and 1998. Hamilton's exhibition went on tour in 2002, after its opening exhibition in Ljubljana in the summer of the previous year, to Tübingen, London, Dublin and Rotterdam.

Lerm Hayes, Christa-Maria. (2004), *Joyce in Art: Visual Art Inspired by James Joyce*. Dublin: Lilliput Press. An exhaustive study that includes many examples of the way *Ulysses* has been treated in modern art; for a shorter essay on the same subject there is an essay by the same author, 'The Joyce Effect: Joyce in Visual Art' in *A Companion to James Joyce*, (ed.) Brown, R. Oxford: Blackwell, pp. 318–40. The best way to enjoy examples of art work inspired by *Ulysses* is by looking through back issues of the *James Joyce Broadsheet* (see page 120). This publication has consistently published illustrative material, often of the kind not previously seen, by artists influenced by their readings of *Ulysses*.

Music From the Works of James Joyce is a CD of music and song, including 'Love's Old Sweet Song', to be sung by Molly Bloom on her Belfast tour with Blazes Boylan and ostensibly to be rehearsed by the two of them on their afternoon liaison; 'Those Lovely Seaside Girls', a ditty that replays itself in Bloom's mind during the course of his day; 'The Croppy Boy' which features in 'Sirens' and a number of other songs. There is also a follow-up *More Music From the Works of James Joyce* and both collections are available from Sunphone Records (www.james-joyce-music.com).

One of the tracks on the first Sunphone recording is 'M'appari', the title song from the Flotow opera *Martha*, which plays a significant role in the 'Sirens' episode. As Simon Dedalus sings the song, at the hour when Molly and Boylan are to meet, Bloom relates each line of it to his life. The song is also available on *JoyceSongs*, recorded by RTÉ in Ireland and released in 2004, and the CD includes other songs referred to in *Ulysses* as well as 'The Sally Gardens', sung by Joyce at a concert in Dublin in 1904 when Nora Barnacle was in the audience. He later wrote out the song's words, from the Yeats poem 'Down by the Sally Gardens', for her. A Canadian documentary film about Joyce and music, *Bloomsday Cabaret*, www.bloomsdaycabaret. com, reflects well the way in which music in *Ulysses* is neither highbrow nor lowbrow but a part of his cultural heritage that was taken for granted.

The influence of *Ulysses* on twentieth-century literature is discussed in detail in Lernout, Geert and Van Mierlo, Wim. eds. (2008), *The Reception of James Joyce in Europe*. London and New York: Continuum. An interesting study of translations of *Ulysses* is found in O'Neill, Patrick. (2005), *Polyglot Joyce: Fictions of Translations*. Toronto: University of Toronto Press. Lawrence, Karen. ed. (1998), *Transcultural Joyce*. Cambridge: Cambridge University Press is a collection of essays reflecting on Joyce's influence on writers from Latin America, South Asia and Europe.

In addition to the novels, poems and films mentioned on pages 99–104, there is also Eagleton, Terry. (1987), *Saints and Scholars*. London: Verso; a piece of comic fiction bringing together in Ireland Leopold Bloom, Wittgenstein, James Connolly and Bakhtin.

The nature of the influence of Joyce on Lacan is the concern of 'Joyce's *Jouissance, or a New Literary Symptom*' in Rabaté, Jean-Michael. (2001), *Jacques Lacan*. Basingstoke: Palgrave.

WEBSITES

www.doc.ic.ac.uk/~rac101/concord/texts/ulysses/ulysses1.html An edition of *Ulysses*, prepared using the Project Gutenberg edition, with a valuable search function.

www.rte.ie/radio1/readingulysses A set of programmes providing an informative, episode-by-episode guide to *Ulysses* with Gerry O Flaherty, a Dublin historian and Joycean, and Fritz Senn, the renowned Swiss Joycean . The last programme in this series features Barry McGovern and Bernard Clarke discussing the role of music in *Ulysses*.

www.antwerpjamesjoycecenter.com Access to the Antwerp James Joyce Centre and its electronic journal (no subscription necessary and all articles available online) devoted to genetic criticism of Joyce's work. While the content is mostly concerned with *Finnegans Wake*, there are articles on *Ulysses* worth consulting, like the publication history of the book in Issue 4, Spring 2004, by Stacey Herbert.

www.joyceimages.com A site dedicated to illustrating Ulysses using period documents.

www.nationalarchives.ie The National Archives of Ireland has a useful range of material relating to Joyce and his fiction.

http://digicoll.library.wisc.edu/JoyceColl Three books on Joyce, currently out of print, are fully accessible: Frank Budgen's *James*

Joyce and the Making of 'Ulysses', C. H. Peake's *James Joyce The Citizen and Artist* and Karen Lawrence's *The Odyssey of Styles in Ulysses.*
www.utulsa.edu/jjq The home page of the *James Joyce Quarterly.*
http://hjs.ff.cuni.cz The homepage of *Hypermedia Joyce Studies.*

SUMMER SCHOOLS, WORKSHOPS AND SYMPOSIA

Up-to-date information on summer schools, workshops, the North American Joyce Conference, the International James Joyce Symposium and other conferences is available online and through the *James Joyce Broadsheet* (see below). For summer schools, lectures, reading groups, walking tours and other *Ulysses*-related events in Ireland, consult the James Joyce Center in Dublin (www.jamesjoyce.ie); for events in North America, including Bloomsday celebrations, consult the James Joyce Society (http://joycesociety.org), the International James Joyce Foundation (http://english.osu.edu/research/organizations/ijjf/) and Bloomsday NYC at www.bloomsdaynyc.org. Information on the James Joyce Summer School held annually at University College Dublin is available at www.joycesummerschool.ie; for the Trieste Joyce School: www2.units.it/~triestejoyce.

JOURNALS

James Joyce Broadsheet is issued three times a year: School of English, University of Leeds, Leeds, LS2 9JT, England.
The *James Joyce Quarterly* was founded in 1963 at the University of Tulsa: www.utulsa.edu/jjq/
The *James Joyce Literary Supplement* is issued through the University of Miami: www.as.miami.edu/english/jjls
The annual *Dublin James Joyce Journal*, the first issue of which appeared in 2008, comes from the University College Dublin James Joyce Research Centre in association with The National Library of Ireland (joyceresearchcentre@ucd.ie)

PAMPHLETS

Also available from the National Library of Ireland (www.nli.ie) is the *Joyce Pamphlets Collection*, 21 issues of the Joyce Studies Series, covering a variety of topics. They serve as a useful introduction to the reading of *Ulysses* and especially relevant are 'Race and Colonialism' by Vincent J. Cheng (No 8), 'Consumption in *Ulysses*' by Kimberly J. Devlin (No 9), 'Beginners' by Margot Norris (No 14) ,'The Rocky Road to *Ulysses*' by Hans Walter Gabler (No 15) and 'Joyce's Modernism' by Sean Latham.

BIBLIOGRAPHY

Adams, R. M. (1962), *Surface and Symbol*. New York: Oxford University Press.

Arnold, Bruce. (2004), *The Scandal of Ulysses*. Dublin: Liffey Press.

Attridge, D. and Ferrer, D. eds. (1984), *Post-Structuralist Joyce*. Cambridge: Cambridge University Press.

Attridge, D. and Howes, M. eds. (2000), *Semicolonial Joyce*. Cambridge: Cambridge University Press.

Attridge Derek, Maud Ellmann, Daniel Ferrer, Andre Topia, Jean-Michel Rabaté and Robert Young. (1986), 'Sirens without Music', in Beja, M. et al. (eds), *James Joyce: The Centennial Symposium*. Urbana: University of Illinois Press, pp. 59–94.

Beckett, Samuel. (1972), 'Dante . . . Bruno . . .Vico . . . Joyce' in Samuel Beckett and Others (eds), *Our Exagmination Round his Factification for Incamination*. London: Faber & Faber.

Broccoli, Matthew J. ed. (1996), *F Scott Fitzgerald on Authorship*. Chapel Hill, NC: University of South Carolina Press.

Budgen, Frank. (1972), *James Joyce and the Making of 'Ulysses'*. Oxford: Oxford University Press.

Cheng, Vincent. (1995), *Joyce, Race and Empire*. New York: Cambridge University Press.

Cixous, Hélène. (1984), 'Joyce: the (R)use of Writing', in D. Attridge and D. Ferrer (eds), *Post-Structuralist Joyce*. Cambridge: Cambridge University Press, pp.15–30.

Deane, Seamus. (1985), 'Joyce and Nationalism', in *Celtic Revivals: Essays in Modern Irish Literature 1880–1980*. London: Faber & Faber, pp. 92–107.

—(1985), 'Joyce and Stephen: the Provincial Intellectual', in *Celtic Revivals: Essays in Modern Irish Literature 1880–1980*. London: Faber & Faber, pp.75–91.

—(1986), ' "Masked with Matthew Arnold's Face": Joyce and Liberalism', in M. Beja (ed.), *James Joyce: The Centennial Symposium*. Urbana, IL: University of Illinois Press.

Deming, Robert. (1970), *James Joyce. The Critical Heritage Vol. 1*. London: Routledge.

Desani, G. V. (1986), *All About H. Hatter*. New York: New York Review Books.

Duffy, Enda. (1994), *The Subaltern 'Ulysses'*. Minneapolis, MN: University of Minnesota Press.

Dylan, Bob. (2004), *Chronicles: Volume One*. London: Simon & Schuster.

Ellmann, Mary. (1968), *Thinking about Women*. New York: Harcourt, Brace and World.

Ellmann, Maud. (2008), '*Ulysses*: The Epic of the Human Body', in Richard Brown (ed.), *A Companion to James Joyce*. Oxford: Blackwell.

Ellmann, Richard. (1972), *Ulysses on the Liffey*. London: Faber & Faber.

—(1982), *James Joyce*: Revised Edition. Oxford: Oxford University Press.

French, Marilyn. (1982), *The Book as World*. London: Abacus.

Gibson, Andrew. (2005), *Joyce's Revenge*. Oxford: Oxford University Press..

—(2006), *James Joyce*: Revised Edition. London: Reaktion Books.

Gibson, A. and Platt, L. (2006) (eds), *Joyce, Ireland, Britain*. Gainesville, FL: Florida University Press.

Gifford, Don and Seidman, Robert J. (2008), *Ulysses Annotated*. Berkeley, CA: University of California Press.

Gilbert, Stuart. (1969), *James Joyce's Ulysses: A Study*. London: Penguin.

Groden, Michael. (1977), *Ulysses in Progress*. Princeton, NJ: Princeton University Press.

Gunn, I. and Hart, C. (2004), *James Joyce's Dublin: A Topographical Guide to the Dublin of Ulysses*. London: Thames & Hudson.

Hamilton, Richard. (2001), *Imaging James Joyce's Ulysses*. London: The British Council.

Hart, Clive and Hayman, David. eds. (1974), *James Joyce's 'Ulysses': Critical Essays*. Berkeley and Los Angeles, CA: University of California Press.

Heaney, Seamus. (1972), *Wintering Out*. London: Faber & Faber.

—(1995), *The Redress of Poetry: Oxford Lectures*. London: Faber & Faber.

—(1998), *Opened Ground*. London: Faber & Faber.

Henke, Suzette A. (1986), 'Virginia Woolf Reads James Joyce: The *Ulysses Notebook*', in Beja, M. et al. (eds), *James Joyce: The Centennial Symposium*. Urbana, IL: University of Illinois Press, pp. 39–42.

Jenkyns, Richard. (1980), *The Victorians and Ancient Greece*. Oxford: Oxford University Press.

Joyce, James. (1957) *Letters of James Joyce*, vol i, ed. Stuart Gilbert. London: Faber & Faber.

—(1966) *Letters of James Joyce*, vol ii and iii, ed. Richard Ellmann. London: Faber & Faber.

—(1975) *Selected Letters of James Joyce*, ed. Richard Ellmann. London: Faber & Faber.

—(2000a), *A Portrait of the Artist as a Young Man*. Oxford: Oxford University Press.

—(2000b), *Occasional, Critical, and Political Writings*. Oxford: Oxford University Press.

—(2008), *Ulysses*, ed. Hans Walter Gabler. London: The Bodley Head.

Kenner, Hugh. (1978), *Joyce's Voices*. London: Faber & Faber.

—(1987), *Dublin's Joyce*. New York: Columbia University Press.

Kiberd, Declan. (1982), 'The Vulgarity of Heroics: Joyce's *Ulysses*', in Suheil Badi Bushrui (ed.), *James Joyce, An International Perspective: Centenary Essays in Honour of the Late Sir Desmond Cochrane*. Gerrards Cross: Colin Smythe, pp. 156–69.

—(1992), *Ulysses: Annotated Student Edition* (Introduction and Notes). London: Penguin.

—(1996), *Inventing Ireland*. London: Vintage.

—(2009), *Ulysses ans Us: The Art of Everyday Living*. London: Faber & Faber.

Killeen, Terrence. (2005), *Ulysses Unbound*. Bray: Wordwell.

Knowlson, James. (1996), *Damned to Fame: The Life of Samuel Beckett*. London: Bloomsbury.

Lattimore, Richard. (1967), *The Odyssey of Homer*. New York: Harper & Row.

Lawrence, Karen. (1981), *The Odyssey of Style in Ulysses*. Princeton, NJ: Princeton University Press.

Leavis, F. R. (1933), 'James Joyce and the Revolution of the Word.' *Scrutiny*, ii.2, pp. 193–201.

Litz, A. Walton. (1964), *The Art of James Joyce*. New York: Oxford University Press.

Lloyd, David. (1993), *Anomalous States: Irish Writing and the Post-Colonial Moment*. Durham, NC: Duke University Press.

MacCabe, Colin. (1979), *James Joyce & The Revolution of the Word*. London: Macmillan.

Mahaffey, Vicki. (1988), *Reauthorizing Joyce*. Cambridge: Cambridge University Press.

Marcus, Laura and Nicholls, Peter. eds. (2003), *The Cambridge History of Twentieth-Century English Literature*. Cambridge: Cambridge University Press.

Meade, Declan. ed. (2004), *James Joyce Bloomsday Magazine 2004*. Dublin: The James Joyce Centre.

Mitchell, Breon. (1976), *James Joyce and the German Novel: 1922–1933*. Athens: Ohio University Press.

Nolan, Emer. (1995), *James Joyce and Nationalism*. London and New York: Routledge.

Norris, Margot. (2004), *Ulysses*. Cork: Cork University Press.

Osteen, Mark. (1992), 'The money question at the back of everything: clichés, counterfeits & forgeries in Joyce's "Eumaeus".' *Modern Fiction Studies*, 38.4, p. 832.

Paulin, Tom. (1984), 'The British Presence in *Ulysses*', in *Ireland & The English Crisis*. Newcastle upon Tyne: Bloodaxe Books.

Peake, C. H. (1977), *James Joyce The Citizen and Artist*. London: Edward Arnold.

Pindar, Ian. (2004), *Joyce*. London: Haus Publishing.

Platt, Len. (1998), *Joyce and the Anglo-Irish: A Study of Joyce and the Literary Revival*. Amsterdam: Rodolpi.

Power, Arthur. (1967) *The Joyce We Knew*, ed. Ulick Connor. Cork: Mercier Press.

—(1974), *Conversations with James Joyce*, ed. Clive Hart. London: Millington.

Quinn, Antoinette. ed. (2004) *Kavanagh, Patrick: Collected Poems*. London: Allen Lane, p. 176.

Read, Forest. (1967), *Pound/Joyce: The Letter of Ezra Pound to James Joyce, With Pound's Essay on Joyce*. London: Faber & Faber.

Rice, Thomas Jackson. (2008), *Cannibal Joyce*. Gainesville, FL: University Press of Florida.

Rose, Danis and O'Hanlon, John. eds. (1989), *The Lost Notebook*. Edinburgh: Split Pea Press.

Schwarz, Daniel R. (1987), *Reading Joyce's Ulysses*. London: Macmillan.

Scott, Bonnie Kime. (1987), *James Joyce*. Brighton: The Harvester Press.

Seidel, Michael. (1976), *Epic Geography*. Princeton, NJ: Princeton University Press.

Sen, Krishna. (2008), 'Where Agni Araflammed and Shiva Slew: Joyce's Interface with India', in Brown R. (ed.), *A Companion to James Joyce*. Oxford: Blackwell, pp. 207–222.

Senn, Fritz. (2007), *Joycean Murmoirs*. Dublin: Lilliput.

Travis, Alan. (2000), *Bound and Gagged: A Secret History of Obscenity in Britain*. London: Profile Books.

Vico, Giambattista. (2001), *New Science*. London: Penguin.

Williams, Keith. (2003), '*Ulysses* in Toontown: "Vision Animated to Bursting Point" in Joyce's "Circe"', in Julian Murphet and Lydia Rainsford (eds), *Literature and Visual Technologies: Writing After Cinema*. Basingstoke: Palgrave Macmillan, pp. 96–121.

Wilson, Edmund. (1966), *Axel's Castle*. London: Fontana.

Wittgenstein, Ludwig. (1961), *Tractatus Logico-Philosophicus*. London: Routledge.

NOTES

CHAPTER 1

1. Joyce (1975), p. 30.
2. Joyce (1966), vol ii, p. 48.
3. Quoted in Pindar (2004), p. 134.

CHAPTER 2

1. Quoted in Henke (1986), p. 40.
2. Dylan (2004), p. 130.
3. Joyce (1966), vol iii, p. 99.
4. Budgen (1972), p. 55
5. Peake (1977), p. 285.
6. Beckett (1972), p. 13.
7. Joyce (1957), p. 129.
8. Joyce (1957), p. 145.
9. Budgen (1972), p. 21.
10. Ibid.
11. Wittgenstein (1961), p. 74.
12. Power (1967), p. 107.
13. Ellmann (1982), p. 397.
14. Ibid., p. 340.
15. Vico (2001), p. 359.
16. Jenkyns (1980).
17. Joyce (1957), p. 175.
18. Ellmann, Maud (2008), p. 66.
19. Ellmann (1982), pp. 523–4.
20. Power (1974), p. 95.
21. Meade (2004), p. 44.

CHAPTER 3

1. Kenner (1978), p. 69.
2. Lawrence (1981), pp. 38–49.
3. Gibson (2005), pp. 32–6.

4. Adams (1962), pp. 18–25, unpacks Deasy's assertions and shows how erroneous his judgements are.
5. The phrase was used by Joyce, to describe how Oscar Wilde (and other Irish writers like Sheridan, Goldsmith and Shaw) was received and assimilated by the English. Joyce (2000b), p. 149. In 'Circe', Mulligan appears in a jester's costume (15.4166–7).
6. Cixous (1984), p. 19.
7. An alternative way of reading the riddle and its 'answer' is to assume there is a buried significance which needs digging out – and there is no shortage of literary truffle-hounds on the scent – but a convincing explanation has yet to surface.
8. Gunn and Hart (2004), pp. 28–30.
9. Budgen (1972), p. 52 and p. 107.
10. Lattimore (1967), p. 139–40 (lines 82–104).
11. For a different example of how more than one narrative voice operates in this chapter see Kenner (1978), p. 73–4.
12. Ellmann (1972), p. 53.
13. Gilbert (1969), pp. 172–6, lists them all.
14. Various interpretations of Stephen's parable are possible because its significance is not obvious but its decidedly un-rhetorical style tells of disappointment and failure and MacHugh is able to pick up on and appreciate the sense of unfulfillment it expresses (7.1035–7, 1061).
15. Joyce (2000b), p. 126.
16. Budgen (1972), p. 20.
17. MacCabe (1979), p. 121.
18. Gibson (2005), pp. 60–80; Platt (1998), pp. 73–86.
19. 'Wandering Rocks' in Hart and Hayman (1974).
20. Budgen (1972), pp. 124–5.
21. An observation mirrored in the vocabulary of J. P. Mahaffy, once the provost of Trinity College Dublin, who saw *Ulysses* as proof that 'it was a mistake to establish a separate university for the aborigines of the island' (quoted in Kiberd (1996), p. 327).
22. Gibson (2005), pp. 81–102; Platt (1998), pp. 86–98.
23. Lawrence (1981), pp. 90–100.
24. Attridge et al (1984); MacCabe (1979), pp. 79–103.
25. Nolan (1995), pp. 62–8.
26. Kenner (1987), p. 255; Lawrence (1981), pp. 101–19; Platt (1998), pp. 142–56; Gibson (2005), pp. 103–26.
27. Budgen (1972), p. 210.
28. 'So completely is Gerty absorbed into this verbal universe that her very reality is in question.' Killeen (2005), pp. 152–3.
29. Scott, Bonnie Kime (1987), pp. 66–7.
30. 'not only haughtiness, arrogance, but is also slang for wide awake, up to the job': Gifford and Seidman (2008), p. 385.
31. Power (1974), p. 98.
32. Joyce (1957), p. 140.
33. Ellmann (1972), p. 136.

34. The authors being used by Joyce are identified, along with examples of the extracts from their writing that appeared in Sainsbury's and Peacock's anthologies, in 'The Oxen of the Sun', James S. Atherton, in Hart and Hayman (1974).
35. A detailed example of how Joyce worked on his material and fashioned it to his own creative end can be found in Hugh Kenner's *Joyce's Voices*, pp.106–9, when he takes a passage from Macaulay in Sainsbury's anthology and compares it with Joyce's 'version' in 'Oxen of the Sun'.
36. Joyce (1957), p. 139.
37. A man in a macintosh was seen on the street during the viceroy's procession (10.1271–2), is mentioned again in 'Cyclops' (12.1497–8) and is spotted by Stephen at the end of 'Oxen of the Sun' (14.1546). Preparing for bed, the man's presence continues to haunt Bloom's mind: 'Who was M'Intosh?' (17.2066).
38. Kenner (1978), p. 93.
39. Gibson (2005), p. 192.
40. Williams (2003).
41. French (1982), p. 211.
42. Osteen (1992).
43. Joyce (1957), pp.159–60.
44. Schwarz (1987), p. 250.
45. Peake (1977), p. 297.
46. Power (1974), p. 54.
47. Ellmann (1968), pp. 74–5.
48. For an illuminating account of 'Penelope' along these lines, see Mahaffey (1988), pp. 175–81.
49. Kiberd (1992), p. 1181.
50. Joyce (1957), p. 171.
51. Kathleen Kearney appears as a character in 'A Mother' in *Dubliners*. She attempts to launch her daughter's concert career by presenting herself as a supporter of the Irish Literary Revival.
52. Joyce (1957), pp. 151–2.
53. MacCabe (1979), p. 132.

CHAPTER 4

1. Arnold (2004).
2. Deming (1970), pp. 268–71. All quotations from Eliot's essay are taken from these pages.
3. Read (1967), p. 136 and p. 250.
4. Ibid., p. 158.
5. Ellmann (1982), p. 667.
6. Wilson (1966), p. 164.
7. Ellmann (1972), p. 2.
8. French (1982), p. 4.
9. Kenner (1978), p. 18.
10. Ibid., p. 41.

11. Ibid., p. 43.
12. Ibid., p. 52.
13. Stephen Heath, 'Ambiviolences: Notes For Reading Joyce' in Attridge, D. and Ferrer, D. (1984), pp. 31–69.
14. Joyce (1966), vol. ii, p. 134.
15. Stephen Heath, 'Ambiviolences: Notes For Reading Joyce' in Attridge, D. and Ferrer, D. (1984), p. 41.
16. F. R. Leavis, 'James Joyce and the Revolution of the Word', in *Scrutiny*, vol ii, no. 2 (1933), pp. 193–201.
17. Lawrence (1981), p. 9.
18. MacCabe (1979), p. 153.
19. Joyce (2000a), p. 159.
20. Kiberd (1982), Paulin (1984), Deane (1985).
21. Cheng (1995), p. 248.
22. Gibson (2006), p. 129.
23. Quoted in Travis (2000), p. 22.
24. Rose and O'Hanlon (1989).

CHAPTER 5

1. Henke (1986), p. 39.
2. Broccoli (1996), p. 91.
3. Sen (2008), p. 220.
4. Desani (1986), p. 10.
5. Marcus and Nicholls (2003), p. 343.
6. Mitchell (1976).
7. Knowlson (1996), p. 282
8. Ibid., p. 160.
9. Heaney (1998), p. 267.
10. Heaney (1972), pp. 31–2.
11. Heaney (1995), p. 199.
12. Meade (2004), p. 29.
13. Ellmann (1982), p. 654.
14. Hamilton (2001), p. 19.
15. Ibid., p. 6.
16. Rice (2008).
17. Quinn, Antoinette., ed, (2004) *Kavanagh, Patrick: Collected Poems*. London: Allen Lane, p. 176.
18. Senn (2007).

INDEX